How to Use This Book

Look for these special features in this book:

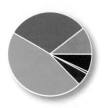

SIDEBARS, **CHARTS**, **GRAPHS**, and original **MAPS** expand your understanding of what's being discussed—and also make useful sources for classroom reports.

FAQs answer common **F**requently **A**sked **Q**uestions about people, places, and things.

WOW FACTORS offer "Who knew?" facts to keep you thinking.

TRAVEL GUIDE gives you tips on exploring the state—either in person or right from your chair!

PROJECT ROOM provides fun ideas for school assignments and incredible research projects. Plus, there's a guide to primary sources—what they are and how to cite them.

Please note: All statistics are as up-to-date as possible at the time of publication.

Consultant: Jennifer Fish Kashay, Professor of Hawaiian History, Colorado State University; William Loren Katz; Scott Rowland, Department of Geology and Geophysics, University of Hawai'i at Manoa

Book production by The Design Lab

Library of Congress Cataloging-in-Publication Data
Kent, Deborah.
 Hawai'i / by Deborah Kent.
    p. cm.—(America the beautiful. Third series)
 Includes bibliographical references and index.
 ISBN-13: 978-0-531-18573-5
 ISBN-10: 0-531-18573-7
 1. Hawai'i—Juvenile literature. I. Title. II. Series.
 DU623.25.K45 2008
 996.9—dc22   2007005705

AMERICA ★ THE ★ BEAUTIFUL

Hawai'i

BY DEBORAH KENT

Third Series

Children's Press®
An Imprint of Scholastic Inc.
New York ★ Toronto ★ London ★ Auckland ★ Sydney
Mexico City ★ New Delhi ★ Hong Kong
Danbury, Connecticut

CONTENTS

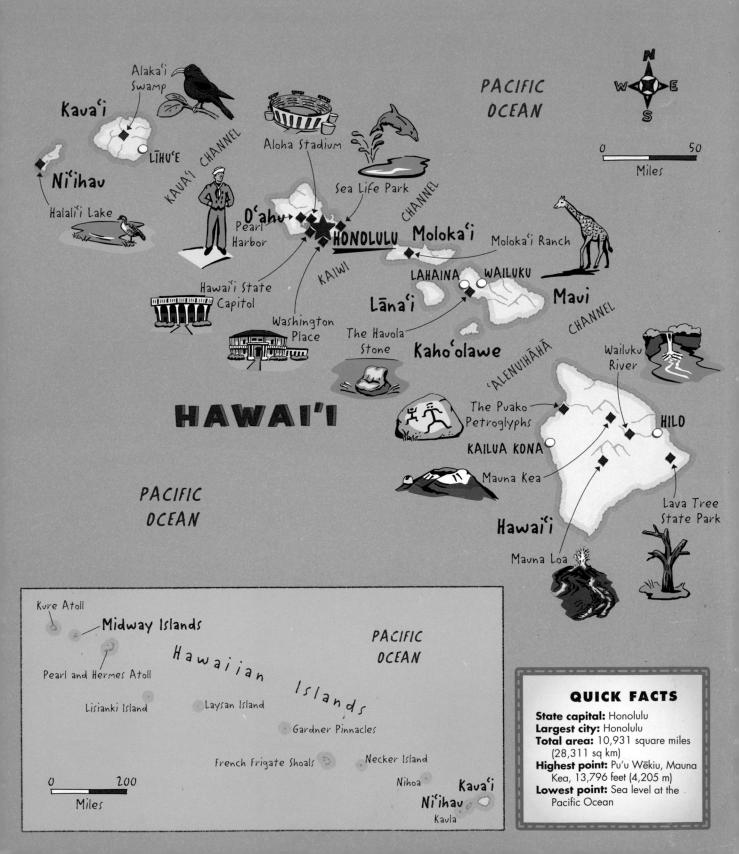

Kaua'i

Alaka'i
Swamp

LĪHU'E

KAUA'I CHANNEL

Ni'ihau

Halali'i Lake

Aloha Stadium

Sea Life Park

PACIFIC
OCEAN

N
W E
S

0   50
Miles

O'ahu

Pearl
Harbor

HONOLULU

Moloka'i

Moloka'i Ranch

CHANNEL

Hawai'i State
Capitol

KAIWI

LAHAINA

WAILUKU

Maui

Lāna'i

The Hauola
Stone

Kaho'olawe

'ALENUIHĀHĀ   CHANNEL

Washington
Place

HAWAI'I

PACIFIC
OCEAN

Wailuku
River

The Puako
Petroglyphs

KAILUA KONA

Mauna Kea

HILO

Lava Tree
State Park

Hawai'i

Mauna Loa

Kure Atoll

Midway Islands

PACIFIC
OCEAN

Hawaiian

Islands

Pearl and Hermes Atoll

Lisianki Island

Laysan Island

Gardner Pinnacles

French Frigate Shoals

Necker Island

Nihoa

Kaua'i

Ni'ihau

Kaula

0   200
Miles

QUICK FACTS

State capital: Honolulu
Largest city: Honolulu
Total area: 10,931 square miles
(28,311 sq km)
Highest point: Pu'u Wēkiu, Mauna
Kea, 13,796 feet (4,205 m)
Lowest point: Sea level at the
Pacific Ocean

Welcome to Hawai'i!

HOW DID HAWAI'I GET ITS NAME?

When we look for the story of Hawai'i's name, we have to reach far into the state's past. According to an ancient story, a Polynesian chief named Hawai'i-Loa set out from his homeland with a band of followers. They crossed the ocean in canoes and came to a string of islands. Hawai'i-Loa and his people settled the islands, which bear the chief's name today.

Other people think the name comes from the Polynesian words *hawaiki* or *owyhyhee*. These words mean "homeland," and may refer to the island from which the early settlers set sail.

Whatever the origin, we know the name comes from the Polynesian language. It is fitting that the state's name reflects the lives of the first people who lived there.

READ ABOUT

A boat sails on the
Pacific Ocean off
the coast of O'ahu.

C H A P T E R O N E

LAND

★

AMONG THE 50 STATES, HAWAI'I IS UNIQUE. Its 10,931 square miles (28,311 square kilometers) are composed entirely of islands. And of the 50 states, only Hawai'i was created by volcanic eruptions. Hawai'i has subtropical rain forests, sandy beaches, and mountains capped with snow. Mauna Kea, the highest point in the state, towers at 13,796 feet (4,205 meters) above sea level. Far below, waves lap the land along the coast.

THE ISLAND STATE

Hawai'i lies in the northern part of the Pacific Ocean, about 2,300 miles (3,700 km) from the North American mainland. It is a chain of 132 large and small islands, sparkling like a necklace among the ocean waves.

The Hawaiian **archipelago** stretches some 1,523 miles (2,451 km), running roughly southeast to northwest. Most of Hawai'i's islands are very tiny. Many are just bits of rock and coral jutting out of the sea.

Hawai'i's eight largest islands all lie at the southeastern end of the archipelago. Starting in the southeast they are Hawai'i, Kaho'olawe, Maui, Lāna'i, Moloka'i, O'ahu, Kaua'i, and Ni'ihau.

WORD TO KNOW

archipelago *chain of islands*

Hawai'i Geo-Facts

Along with the state's geographical highlights, this chart ranks Hawai'i's land, water, and total area compared to all other states.

Total area; rank . . . . 10,931 square miles (28,311 sq km); 43rd
Land; rank . . . . 6,423 square miles (16,635 sq km); 47th
Water; rank . . . . 4,508 square miles (11,675 sq km); 13th
Inland water; rank . . . . 38 square miles (98 sq km); 50th
Coastal water; rank . . . . 590 square miles (1,528 sq km); 10th
Territorial water; rank . . . . . . 4,470 square miles (11,577 km); 4th
Geographic center In the ocean, southwest of Moloka'i and west of Lāna'i
Latitude . . . . 16° 55' N to 23° N
Longitude . . . . 154° 40' W to 162° W
Highest point . . . . Pu'u Wēkiu, Mauna Kea, 13,796 feet (4,205 m)
Lowest point . . . . Sea level at the Pacific Ocean
Largest city . . . . Honolulu
Longest river . . . . Wailua and Waimea rivers on Kaua'i; Wailuku River on Hawai'i; and Kaukonahua Stream on O'ahu, none of which is longer than 50 miles (80 km)

Source: U.S. Census Bureau

 Based on total land area, the islands of Hawai'i would fit inside Texas more than 24 times.

The islands that make up Hawai'i are so small that the state has no long rivers. The 26-mile (42 km) Wailuku River on the island of Hawai'i is the longest river in the state. The largest lake in Hawai'i is Halali'i Lake on Ni'ihau. It covers 182 acres (74 hectares) of land.

Although Hawai'i is only 47th in area among the states, it stretches a long way—523 miles (2,452 km). California, the third-largest state, stretches only 1,200 miles (1,932 km)!

Hawai'i's Topography

Use the color-coded elevation chart to see on the map Hawai'i's high points (dark red to orange) and low points (green to dark green). Elevation is measured as the distance above or below sea level.

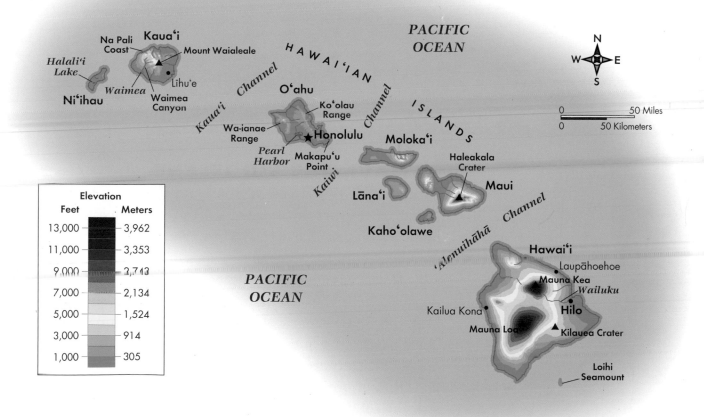

Tourists enjoy a view of the Pacific Ocean from Oʻahu.

HAWAIʻI, THE BIG ISLAND

Because it is the largest of the Hawaiian Islands, the island of Hawaiʻi is often called the Big Island. It is home to Kīlauea, one of the most active volcanoes in the world. With their spectacular scenes of cliffs and waterfalls, Hawaiʻi's mountainous areas are a photographer's delight. The highest of the mountainous areas, particularly the upper slopes of Mauna Loa and Mauna Kea, don't have cliffs and waterfalls. This is because they are geologically too young and they extend above the elevation of greatest rainfall. The island also has wide stretches of grassland where thousands of cattle graze.

MAUI, KAHO'OLAWE, LĀNA'I, AND MOLOKA'I

The island of Maui lies northwest of Hawai'i. It is separated from Hawai'i by the 'Alenuihāhā Channel. Snuggled close to Maui are the three much smaller islands of Moloka'i, Lāna'i, and Kaho'olawe.

Maui is the second-largest of the Hawaiian Islands. Haleakalā Volcano soars in the southeastern part of the island. Below it spreads the great Haleakalā Crater, carved by streams and waterfalls. Northern Maui is a rugged region of mountains and forests.

Kaho'olawe is a small, barren island with no towns or villages. Moloka'i is a long, narrow island with tall cliffs on its northern shore. The western end of Moloka'i is low and dry. Lāna'i used to be called the Pineapple Island. At one time, nearly all of the land was used for raising pineapples.

O'AHU

The island of O'ahu is built of two mountain ranges. The Ko'olau Mountains form the northeastern part of the island. On the southwestern side is the Wa'ianae Range. Between these two mountain chains is a broad plateau. The coast of O'ahu has some of the most beautiful beaches anywhere in the islands.

KAUA'I AND NI'IHAU

The central portion of Kaua'i is a wild region of swamps and deep, narrow valleys. The Nā Pali Cliffs along the northwest coast are dizzyingly magnificent. The Waimea Canyon of the Waimea River is often called the Grand Canyon of the Pacific. Halali'i Lake, on tiny Ni'ihau, is the biggest lake in the state. It covers 82 acres (74 ha). By the standards of most states, it isn't

Lava from Kīlauea, one of Hawai'i's three active volcanoes, flows into the Pacific Ocean.

WORDS TO KNOW

molten *hot enough to melt*

lava *melted, or molten, rock that comes from a volcano*

Hawai'i's Mauna Kea is the tallest mountain on Earth. It rises more than 33,000 feet (10,065 m) from the ocean floor. The top of the mountain stands 13,796 feet (4,205 m) above sea level.

much more than a pond! Although Ni'ihau is one of the smallest of the main islands today, it is actually the remnant of what was once a much larger island.

AN UNEASY PARADISE

Many of the coasts of Hawai'i's islands are covered with palm trees and a dazzling array of flowers. The air is balmy all year long, and the ocean that laps the beaches is always warm. Above 4,000 feet (1,220 m) the air is cooler. With its natural beauty, Hawai'i appears to be a kind of earthly paradise.

Yet nature in Hawai'i is anything but gentle. The Hawaiian Islands were formed over millions of years by a series of volcanic eruptions. **Molten lava** erupted from cracks in the ocean floor and slowly built up to form undersea mountains. Eventually, these mountains grew high enough to emerge from the water as islands.

Most of Hawai'i's volcanoes are extinct today, meaning that they no longer erupt. Hawai'i has only three

SHIELD VOLCANOES AND STRATOVOLCANOES

Hawai'i's volcanoes are wide at the base and rise to a summit that is relatively flat. Geologists call them shield volcanoes. Shield volcanoes are created when the lava that is erupting is very fluid (geologists say it has a low viscosity). If the lava has a low viscosity, it cannot pile up steeply. On the other hand, cone-shaped volcanoes, usually called stratovolcanoes or composite volcanoes, are formed when **magma** is not fluid (it has a high viscosity). This means that the erupted lava can pile up in steep blobs and also that the eruptions tend to be much more violent. These eruptions produce large amounts of volcanic ash, which can also pile up steeply.

WORDS TO KNOW

magma *melted rock that has not yet erupted*

tsunamis *huge waves caused by undersea or near-shore earthquakes, eruptions, or landslides*

active volcanoes. These are Kīlauea, Mauna Loa, and Lo'ihi.

Every year, thousands of earthquakes rattle the island of Hawai'i. Some of these quakes are associated with eruptions of Hawai'i's volcanoes. Most earthquakes are very small. You might feel a slight shudder beneath your feet. Then everything settles back to normal again.

Sometimes very serious earthquakes occur in Hawai'i. On April 2, 1868, a giant quake destroyed 100 homes and killed 81 people.

Even an earthquake thousands of miles away can be deadly in Hawai'i. Some quakes trigger huge rushing waves called **tsunamis**. Tsunamis have been known to cross the Pacific in just a few hours and crash on Hawai'i's shorelines. Tsunamis also have been known to reach upwards of 60 feet (18 m) high and crash inland as far as a quarter mile (.4 km), causing devastation to the surrounding areas. About

SEE IT HERE!

HAWAI'I VOLCANOES NATIONAL PARK

Watching streams of lava slide down the sides of a volcano is but one of many amazing attractions at Hawai'i Volcanoes National Park on the island of Hawai'i. The park covers some 333,000 acres (134,865 ha) and includes two of Hawai'i's active volcanoes, Mauna Loa and Kīlauea. If lava flows far enough, it enters the ocean, sending up clouds of steam. Molten lava enters the water at 2,100 degrees Fahrenheit (1,140 degrees Celsius). Lava-watching is thrilling, but you must stand at a safe distance and follow all the park's precautions.

More than half of the park is a wilderness area, with hiking trails and campsites. Hiking over volcanic rock is a real challenge. Some lava rocks can be razor sharp.

Q8 WHAT ARE THE WORST EARTHQUAKES IN HAWAI'I'S HISTORY?

A8 Two of the worst include one on April 2, 1868, in southern Hawai'i—it killed 81 people and destroyed 100 homes—and one on October 15, 2006, near Kīholo Bay, Hawai'i, which destroyed $100 million worth of property.

50 tsunamis have struck Hawai'i since the early 1800s. The worst tsunami on record hit the Big Island on April 1, 1946. It killed 170 people in the towns of Hilo and Laupāhoehoe.

CLIMATE

The temperature in Hawai'i is mild throughout the year. It rarely has extremes of heat or cold. Scientists call this type of climate subtropical. In both summer and winter, the temperature hovers in the 70s and low 80s. The climate is warmest near sea level. In the mountains, the days and nights tend to be somewhat cooler. During most winters, Hawai'i's tallest mountains are capped with snow. From January to March, there is even enough snow on Mauna Kea for downhill skiing!

However, the weather in Hawai'i can bring some surprises. Fierce tropical storms called hurricanes form in the ocean to the south each year. Rarely, a hurricane roars northward to the Hawaiian Islands. On September 11, 1992, Hurricane Iniki ripped across the island of Kaua'i with winds of 130 miles (209 km) per hour. Iniki was one of the worst hurricanes in Hawai'i's history. It uprooted trees, flattened homes, and washed away crops. The storm caused $2.3 billion in property damage. Since statehood, however, only three hurricanes have hit the Hawaiian Islands directly.

Weather Report

TEMPERATURE 100°F   **TEMPERATURE** 12°F

This chart shows record temperatures (high and low) for the state, as well as average temperatures (July and January) and average annual precipitation.

Record high temperature . . . . 100°F (38°C)
at Pahala on April 27, 1931
Record low temperature . . . . .12°F (–11°C)
at Mauna Kea on May 17, 1979
Average July temperature . . . . 81°F (27°C)
Average January temperature . . . . 73°F (22°C)
Average annual precipitation . . . . 18 inches (45 cm)

Source: National Climatic Data Center, NESDIS, NOAA, U.S. Department of Commerce

ANIMAL LIFE

Isolated from the rest of the world, many unique animals evolved on the Hawaiian Islands. Fish swam in the rivers and streams, and the forests were loud with birdsong. The only way new animals reached Hawai'i was by flying, swimming, or drifting on logs. Prior to the arrival of humans, Hawai'i had no rodents or grazing animals. Its only native mammals are bats and sea creatures such as seals, dolphins, and whales.

Nearly all of the animals that live in Hawai'i today were introduced from other parts of the world. **Alien** species have crowded out most of the species native to Hawai'i. **Feral** pigs and goats damage fragile forests. Rats and mice eat the seeds of native plants. A weasel-like mammal called the mongoose, native to Asia,

HAWAI'I'S ENDANGERED SPECIES

Hawai'i has the distinction of being called the Endangered Species Capital of the World. More than 100 of the state's plants and animals are listed as endangered or threatened. Per square mile, Hawai'i has more endangered species than any other place in the world. Endangered mammals and birds include the Hawaiian hoary bat, Hawaiian monk seal, Moloka'i creeper, Hawaiian crow, Laysan duck, and the nēnē, or Hawaiian goose. Among the endangered plants are several species of fern and silversword.

WORDS TO KNOW

alien *foreign*

feral *once domesticated but now gone back to the wild*

A humpback whale leaps out of the Pacific Ocean.

Hawai'i National Park Areas

This map shows some of Hawai'i's national parks, monuments, preserves, and other areas protected by the **National Park Service.**

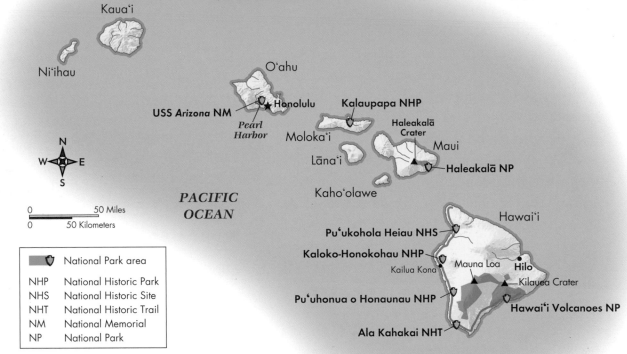

Kaua'i

Ni'ihau

O'ahu

USS Arizona NM

Honolulu

Pearl Harbor

Kalaupapa NHP

Moloka'i

Haleakalā Crater

Lāna'i

Maui

Haleakalā NP

PACIFIC OCEAN

Kaho'olawe

Hawai'i

Pu'ukohola Heiau NHS

Kaloko-Honokohau NHP

Kailua Kona

Mauna Loa

Hilo

Kilauea Crater

Pu'uhonua o Honaunau NHP

Hawai'i Volcanoes NP

Ala Kahakai NHT

0 — 50 Miles
0 — 50 Kilometers

	National Park area
NHP	National Historic Park
NHS	National Historic Site
NHT	National Historic Trail
NM	National Memorial
NP	National Park

N
W E
S

THE NĒNĒ, HAWAI'I'S STATE BIRD

During the 1940s, hunters drove the nēnē to the brink of extinction. In the 1950s, Hawai'i launched efforts to save this unique bird. Nēnēs were raised in captivity and released in the wild. Today, there are about 800 wild nēnēs on Hawai'i, Maui, and Kaua'i.

A nēnē on Maui

was brought to Hawai'i to kill rats. The mongoose now thrives in the islands and eats the eggs and young of native birds.

Most of the animals native to Hawai'i are found nowhere else on Earth. Hawai'i has 3,750 native insect species, 1,064 kinds of land snails, and 71 bird species.

MINI-BIO

DONNA KAHAKUI: CARING FOR THE SEA

As a child in Waikīkī, Donna Kahakui (1964—) enjoyed swimming in the ocean. As the years passed, however, pollution began to affect the ocean. She realized that people must learn to care for the sea. She founded an organization called Kai Makana (gift from the sea) to teach the public about preserving ocean resources. Kahakui publicized her work by paddling among the islands in a canoe. In 1999, she paddled solo 140 miles (225 km) from the Big Island of Hawai'i to O'ahu.

? Want to know more? See http://starbulletin. com/2007/07/05/news/story04.html

A plumeria blossom

PLANT LIFE

Plants, too, have developed in isolation on the Hawaiian Islands. Hawai'i has 1,729 kinds of flowering plants, most of which can be found nowhere else. However, plants and trees from other parts of the world are now crowding out native flora. Miconia, clidemia, blackberry, and albesia are among the plants that have spread into natural areas and pushed native plants aside.

PROTECTING THE ENVIRONMENT

Hawai'i's residents are increasingly aware of threats to the environment. Environmental groups urge people to avoid polluting the land and sea. Schoolchildren are taught to **mālama**, or care for, the natural world. The state of Hawai'i is working to control feral pigs and goats by fencing protected areas. Many rare plants are being reestablished.

WORD TO KNOW

mālama *Hawaiian word meaning "to care for"*

READ ABOUT

Herb Kawainui
Kane painted
*The Discovery of
Hawai'i*, his vision
of Polynesians
first reaching
Hawai'i.

200–300 CE
*The first Polynesian
voyagers reach Hawai'i*

▲ **1000**
*The first petroglyphs are
carved at Puako*

1200
*A new group of
Polynesians arrives in
Hawai'i*

CHAPTER TWO

FIRST PEOPLE

★

HUMAN BEINGS PROBABLY REACHED HAWAI'I SOMETIME IN THE THIRD OR FOURTH CENTURY CE. They were Polynesians who had lived for thousands of years on islands scattered across the South Pacific. Many historians believe that Hawai'i's earliest settlers came from the islands now known as the Marquesas. Later Hawaiians referred to the first settlers as *ka poe kahiko*, "people of the past."

Late 1200s

Pa'ao arrives in the islands and strengthens the kapu system

fishhook

◄1400s

Many fishing villages are established

1627

Spanish sailors visit Hawai'i

KA POE KAHIKO

The ancient Polynesians were skilled seafarers. Without compasses or maps, they charted their position at sea by studying the stars. They traveled thousands of miles in great canoes carved from mahogany logs. Their canoes had billowing sails woven from strips of bark.

The Polynesians brought along everything they needed for life on the Hawaiian Islands. Their canoes were loaded with pigs, dogs, and chickens. They also brought the seeds and sprouts of food plants. To Hawai'i they introduced banana, coconut, **taro**, and **breadfruit** plants. The newcomers built their first villages on the islands of Hawai'i and Kaua'i. From there, they spread to the other islands of the Hawaiian chain.

Some historians believe that a second wave of Polynesian people reached Hawai'i sometime around the year 1200. They may have come from the island of Tahiti. The Tahitians defeated and absorbed the earlier settlers. They were unusually tall people and were noted for their strength. Men often stood over 6 feet (183 centimeters) in height. Among the new colonists were poets, skilled weavers, healers, and builders. There were also priests, or **kahunas**, who led the people in important religious rituals.

WORDS TO KNOW

taro *a vegetable similar to the beet, with leaves and roots that are edible when cooked*

breadfruit *a large, starchy fruit that grows on trees*

kahunas *Hawaiian word for "priests"*

Kahunas were often experts in a certain subject or skill, such as navigation, astronomy, or carving.

Native American Peoples

(Before European Contact)

This map shows the general area of Native people before Europeans arrived.

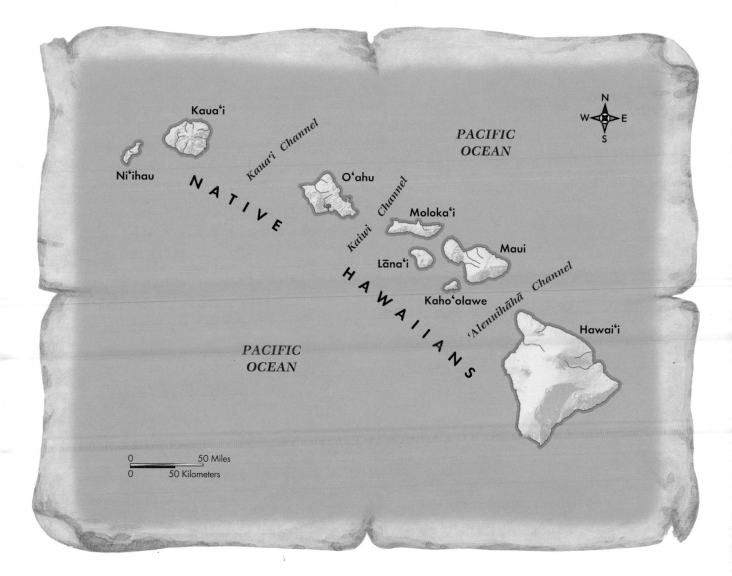

THE POWER OF THE GODS

The Hawaiians believed that many gods and goddesses controlled the world and that the ali'i were the gods' descendants. Sacred ancestors passed their power to the ali'i. This god-given power was known as **mana**. All people had mana, but the mana of the ali'i was by far the strongest.

WORDS TO KNOW

mana *Hawaiian word for "power given by the gods"*

maka'aina *Hawaiian word for "commoners"*

ali'i *Hawaiian word for "chiefs"*

CHIEFS, PRIESTS, COMMONERS, AND SLAVES

In Hawaiian society, everyone knew his or her place. People were born into a particular class and remained there throughout their lives.

The majority of the people belonged to the class of **maka'aina**, or commoners. They were farmers, fishers, and craftspeople. The social class below the commoners was the slaves, mostly captives taken in warfare. The social class above the commoners was the kahunas. This class included the priests. The kahunas passed their special knowledge to their children.

The **ali'i**, or chiefs, ruled Hawaiian society. A head chief, or ali'i nui, might have several lesser chieftains under him. Chiefs and chieftains (both male and female) were entitled to have many spouses. The ali'i had tremendous power and commanded total obedi-

In early Hawaiian society, men were responsible for providing food as well as cooking it.

ence. The chief lived in a special house raised above the rest of the village on a stone platform. Hanging in front of the chief's house were banners of brightly colored feathers.

From the time they were children, Hawaiians learned to respect the gods and goddesses. They kept

A carving of Ku, the Hawaiian god of war

PA'AO: LAYING DOWN THE RULES

Hundreds of years after the first settlers sailed to Hawai'i, a kahuna visited from the islands to the south. According to Hawaiian legend, he was named Pa'ao. Pa'ao thought the Hawaiians had grown lax and disrespectful of their chiefs. He laid down many new rules about how the chiefs should be treated. Under Pa'ao's leadership, the social rules became much tighter. Pa'ao is remembered as the most influential kahuna of the Native Hawaiian religion.

FAQ

Q8 WHAT GODS AND GODDESSES DID THE HAWAIIANS WORSHIP?

A8 The Hawaiians worshipped many gods and goddesses. Here is a list of a few of them:
Ku: God of War
Pele: Goddess of Fire
Kūne: God of Life and Light
Lono: God of the Harvest
Hi'iaka: Goddess of Water

them happy with prayers and gifts. Gifts included offerings of fruits, vegetables, fish, and meat. On some occasions, the priests called for human sacrifices as well. Victims were usually prisoners or slaves.

If the gods were pleased, they would protect humans and bring them success. If the gods were angry, they could cause disease, hunger, and defeat in battle.

Another way the Hawaiians kept the gods happy was by following a set of rules called **kapu**. Strong kapu, or taboos, forbade people from doing many things. For instance, it was kapu for men and women to eat together. The Hawaiians believed that a woman would steal a man's mana if she ate with him. It was kapu for a commoner to touch anything belonging to a chief. If a commoner so much as touched an ali'i's shadow, even by accident, the commoner could be put to death! When a chief traveled through a village, his servants ran ahead to warn the people. The villagers threw themselves on the ground to avoid brushing the chief's shadow as he passed.

WORDS TO KNOW

petroglyphs *pictures carved or painted on stone*

kapu *a system of taboos forbidding certain actions*

SEE IT HERE!

ART ON STONE

The Puako **Petroglyphs** in the Kohala District of the island of Hawai'i are a series of 3,000 pictures carved on hills of hardened lava. They were made by many hands between 1000 and 1800 CE. Some of the pictures show warriors and chiefs. Birds appear in other carvings. Some show scenes from legends or glimpses of ordinary life. In one place, you can see a line of 29 figures marching in single file. Where are they going? The answer remains a mystery.

UMI: THE COMMONER CHIEF

Umi (early 1400s) was the most famous chief from early Hawaiian history. His mother was a commoner, but his father was a chief named Liloa. Until he was 10, Umi lived with his mother and was raised as a commoner himself. Eventually, he became chief of the Big Island and reigned for many years. He never forgot his commoner upbringing and would sometimes help the farmers and fishers with their work—which is what made him famous.

EVERYDAY LIFE

Native Hawaiian fishers sometimes used spears in shallow waters to catch fish.

Native Hawaiian boys were taught to fish, farm, and fight. Fishers went out on the ocean in canoes and caught fish with nets and lines. Fishers carefully carved fishhooks from bone, which were very valuable.

Men and boys also hoed, planted, and harvested crops. Each family group had use of its own fields, which were controlled by the ali'i nui. Cooking was also considered men's work. The men cooked in an open pit called an imu. They built a fire there and heated large stones. Then they put in the food and covered it with banana leaves. After the food had steamed in the imu, it was ready to eat.

Although the men did the cooking, women and girls had plenty of work. They were in charge of making fabric and sewing. They would make a cloth

Hawaiian fishhook

WORDS TO KNOW

kapa *fabric made from the inner bark of trees*

malos *garments worn by Hawaiian men over their lower body*

To make kapa, women pounded and flattened softened tree bark.

called **kapa** from the inner bark of trees called wauke. The women printed patterns on the kapa by pressing it with carved stones. They could also paint the kapa in vivid colors. The fabric was used to make women's skirts and **malos** for men. Both men and women sometimes wore jingling ankle bracelets made from shells.

When they went before the public, the chiefs wore extravagant outfits made of feathers. The feathers were woven so tightly that the garment was as smooth as velvet. On his head, the chief wore a feather-covered helmet, sometimes topped by a tall, feathered crest. The startling colors and fierce, high crest made the chief a frightening sight!

FAQ

Q8 DID EACH ISLAND HAVE ITS OWN CHIEF?

A8 A chief might rule one island, or have two or three islands under his control. Sometimes a large island was divided among several chiefs.

Armed Hawaiian warriors prepare for battle.

PEACETIME AND WARFARE

Throughout the islands, the people of Hawai'i lived by the concept of **aloha**. The word aloha was a warm greeting, but it was also much more. It was a spirit of affection and regard. Ho'okipa aloha means hospitable.

The aloha spirit did not keep the Hawaiians from fighting among themselves. Warfare between one island and another was frequent. When war broke out, the chief called on the men and older boys to fight. Hawaiian warriors were skilled in the use of many

WORD TO KNOW

aloha *Hawaiian word of greeting, also meaning a spirit of affection and regard*

A chief's cloak might contain as many as a million feathers collected from thousands of birds!

Picture Yourself . . .

Greeting Visitors to Your Island

It is a hot summer day on the island of Kahoʻolawe. You and your sister go down to the beach for a swim. As you cool yourselves in the waves, you hear the splash of paddles in the distance. Looking up, you see a large canoe making its way toward you. The paddler in front calls a friendly greeting. You don't recognize him. Because he is coming from the northwest, you know that he is from the island of Maui. You and your sister run to the village and announce that strangers have arrived. Everyone rushes to the beach to greet them. Soon a meal of fish is steaming in the imu. There will be an evening of singing and storytelling. You feel glad that you were the first to spot the visitors. You can't wait to learn who they are and why they have traveled so far.

weapons. They threw spears and brandished heavy wooden clubs. They fired sharp-edged lava chunks at their enemies with slingshots.

Hawaiian custom protected women and children when wars raged. The kahunas guarded special refuges that were surrounded by white kapa flags. A strong kapu stopped enemy invaders from harming anyone inside the refuge. A Hawaiian could also use the refuge to escape a personal enemy during peacetime.

Even in the midst of war, Hawaiians looked forward to the yearly harvest festival of Makahiki. Makahiki began sometime in November and lasted three or four months. It started off with rituals in honor of Lono, the god of the harvest. The chiefs went from village to village, collecting taxes from the commoners. Taxes were paid in the form of food, animals, and kapa. At last, when the ceremonies were done and the taxes had been collected, the true celebration began. Makahiki was a joyful time of singing, dancing, and games for everyone.

HAWAIIANS AT PLAY

Early Hawaiians greatly enjoyed games that tested their strength and skill. During Makahiki, spectators gathered to watch boxing and wrestling matches. The best runners competed in footraces. There were spear-throwing contests and competitions to see who could roll a stone the farthest.

Part of the fun was betting on who would win. Spectators bet pigs, chickens, and coconuts. As the excitement mounted, bets went higher and higher. Sometimes a spectator even bet his nets, canoe, or house!

The ocean was all around them, offering wonderful opportunities for recreation. From early childhood, they swam and dove. They learned to ride the waves on long, graceful boards. This ancient Hawaiian sport was an ancestor of today's surfing.

WHITE-SKINNED VISITORS

According to Hawaiian legends, a great canoe with huge sails once sank near the coast of the Big Island. A pale-skinned man and woman survived and swam ashore. To the amazement of the black-haired Hawaiians, the strangers had red hair! The strangers stayed with the Hawaiians and had many children. Their red-haired descendants were called the ehu.

The story of the ehu hinted that other races of people lived far across the sea. The Hawaiians could never have imagined the impact such people would have on their lives and on the future of the islands.

Sports involving the ocean have been popular in Hawai'i for centuries.

SLEDDING, HAWAIIAN STYLE

The Hawaiians invented a way to go sledding without snow. They built steep runways and filled them with smooth stones. Then they slid to the bottom.

READ ABOUT

Native Hawaiians greeted the captain and crew of the *Resolution* off the coast of Kaua'i.

▲ **1778**
Captain James Cook's expedition reaches Hawai'i

1779
In a fight between the British and the Hawaiians, Captain Cook is killed

1790
Chief Kamehameha of the island of Hawai'i begins construction of the Pu'ukohola Temple

CHAPTER THREE

EXPLORATION AND SETTLEMENT

★

O N A JANUARY EVENING IN 1778, A HAWAIIAN FISHER NAMED MOAPU TURNED HIS CANOE TOWARD THE SHORE OF KAUA'I. Suddenly, an astonishing sight glided into view. Two huge shapes were moving toward the island. They looked like mountains that floated on the waves. Above them rippled giant clouds of cloth. Moapu had never seen such enormous sheets of kapa!

1790
Sandlewood becomes an important export

1796 ▶
Kamehameha gains control of Kaho'olawe, O'ahu, Moloka'i, Lāna'i, and Maui

1810
Kamehameha unites all of the islands as the Kingdom of Hawai'i

THE TEMPLES OF LONO

Moapu paddled to shore, ran up the beach, and shouted to the villagers. Within minutes, people crowded the shore. They stared in wonder as the sea mountains drew nearer.

A kahuna told the people that the ships were temples to Lono, the god of the harvest. They had arrived in the middle of Makahiki, the harvest festival. Perhaps one of the ships carried Lono himself!

The chief decided they would have to investigate. He sent several men in canoes to climb aboard the sea temples. He ordered them to learn whatever they could.

The investigators returned with amazing tales. They said they had seen strange creatures with three-cornered heads and skin that hung loosely over their

Hawaiians were celebrating Makahiki when they first spotted the strange object approaching their shores.

Exploration of Hawai'i

The colored arrows on this map show the route taken by James Cook during 1778 and 1779.

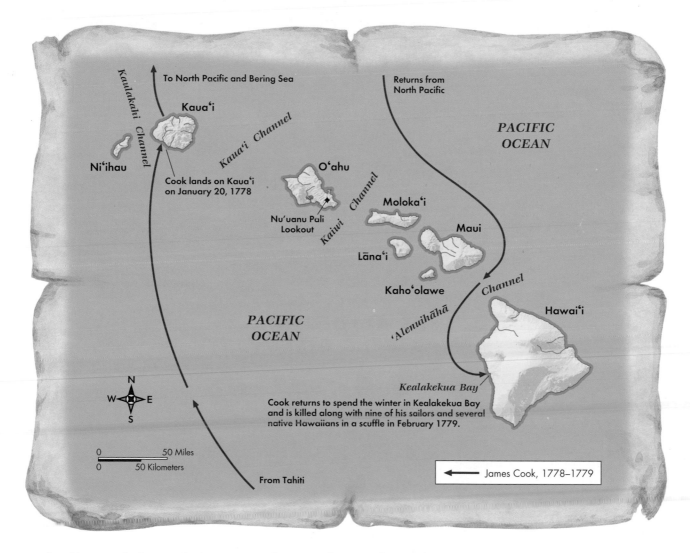

To North Pacific and Bering Sea

Kaulakahi Channel

Kaua'i

Ni'ihau

Kaua'i Channel

Cook lands on Kaua'i
on January 20, 1778

Returns from
North Pacific

**PACIFIC
OCEAN**

O'ahu

Kaiwi Channel

Nu'uanu Pali
Lookout

Moloka'i

Maui

Lāna'i

Kaho'olawe

'Alenuihāhā Channel

Hawai'i

**PACIFIC
OCEAN**

Kealakekua Bay

Cook returns to spend the winter in Kealakekua Bay
and is killed along with nine of his sailors and several
native Hawaiians in a scuffle in February 1779.

N W E S

| 0 | 50 Miles |
| 0 | 50 Kilometers |

From Tahiti

◄———— James Cook, 1778–1779

bodies and formed deep pouches at their sides. The
skin of their feet was thick and tough, and their voices
sounded like the twitter of birds. The men weren't
sure whether these creatures were gods or mortals.
They weren't like any humans that had ever been
seen before!

Initially, the Hawaiians treated Captain Cook and his crew warmly, offering them gifts and food.

IN SEARCH OF THE NORTHWEST PASSAGE

Ever since Columbus stumbled upon the Americas, Europeans had dreamed of a sea route past North America to Asia. The discovery of such a "Northwest Passage" would bring wealth and glory. For nearly three centuries, daring sailors risked their lives to find it. Instead, they found ice and wind, hunger, and sometimes death. There wouldn't be a shortcut through the Americas until 1914, the year that the first ship passed through the Panama Canal.

THE *RESOLUTION* AND THE *DISCOVERY*

The mysterious floating mountains turned out to be two British ships, the HMS *Resolution* and the HMS *Discovery*, commanded by Captain James Cook of the British Royal Navy. Cook was heading north to the Arctic. The Earl of Sandwich in England had sent him on an expedition to find the legendary Northwest Passage.

Cook visited Kaua'i and Ni'ihau for several weeks. He named the islands in honor of the Earl of Sandwich. The islands of Hawai'i became known as the Sandwich Islands.

The brightly colored flowers and sweet, delicious fruits of the islands delighted Cook and his men. Most of all, they were charmed by the friendly Hawaiians. Everywhere they went, people welcomed them with food and gifts.

Finally, Captain Cook ordered his men back to the ships. They set out again on their search for the Northwest Passage. Paddlers from Kaua'i and Ni'ihau rushed to the other islands with news of the strange visitors. For months afterward, no one seemed to talk about anything else.

Ten months after they left, the *Resolution* and the *Discovery* returned to Hawai'i. This time, the ships visited all of the inhabited islands. The Hawaiian chiefs took the visitors to see the weavers who made feather cloaks. They showed them how canoes were carved from mahogany logs. In return, the British took the Hawaiians aboard their ships. They showed them how the ships' blacksmiths made iron tools.

Finally, Cook's ships anchored at Kealakekua Bay on the south coast of the Big Island. Once again, the British received a royal welcome. Some Hawaiians believed that Cook represented Lono.

After a few weeks, however, the welcome wore thin. The visitors gobbled up supplies of food and asked for more. When they needed firewood, they burned the fence around a temple. Cook and his men also repeatedly broke the kapus, frequently eating with Hawaiian women on their ship and serving forbidden foods such as bananas and pork. The Hawaiians looked forward to the time when they would go on their way.

At last, to the relief of their weary hosts, the visitors set sail. But only a week later the ships were back. They had run into a storm and needed to make repairs.

Picture Yourself . . .

Meeting Europeans for the First Time

Carefully, warily, you climb the ladder and step onto the deck of the great ship. Your father is beside you, assuring you that you are safe. One of the pale-skinned strangers shows you a sharp knife. It is made of something hard and shiny. He smiles and tells you with gestures that the knife is a gift. He speaks in his peculiar, chattering language. You thank him and hope he understands. Your father studies the ropes attached to the ship's enormous sails. He tells you he would like to build a giant canoe and work the sails with ropes like these. You imagine sailing far, far across the waves and finding the land of the **haoles**. Perhaps someday you will travel on a great ship like this and visit strange new lands!

WORD TO KNOW

haoles *foreign-born Hawaiian islanders (usually Caucasian)*

MINI-BIO

CAPTAIN JAMES COOK: EXPLORER OF THE WORLD

When he was 17, James Cook (1728–1779) went to work for a shipping company in the English town of Whitby, Yorkshire. Later, he joined the British Royal Navy. In 1768, Cook was appointed captain of a scientific expedition to the Pacific. He and his crew became the first Europeans to see and map the coasts of Australia and South Island of New Zealand. On another voyage, in 1778, he landed in Hawai'i, which he named the Sandwich Islands. In 1779, when tensions began to arise between the English explorer and Native Hawaiians, Cook was killed during a confrontation.

❓ Want to know more? See www.bbc.co.uk/history/ historic_figures/cook_james.shtml

Trouble flared all too soon. A Hawaiian man stole one of the longboats, which the British used for getting from ship to shore. Captain Cook was outraged. He went ashore to punish the thief. A warrior struck Cook with a wooden club, and Cook cried out in pain. The Hawaiians shouted in excitement. If Cook felt pain, he must not be a god after all! Angry warriors surged around him. They knocked him to the ground and beat him to death. In revenge, Cook's men burned the village and killed several of the Hawaiians. Then they sailed away from the islands where they had once been greeted with the spirit of aloha.

About a year after Captain Cook's first visit to the islands, he was killed during a conflict with Native Hawaiians.

THE WORLD FLOODS IN

Captain Cook's sorry end did nothing to discourage foreign visitors. Word of the beautiful Hawaiian Islands spread to Europe, Asia, and the Americas. Over the years that followed, hundreds of foreign ships anchored off the islands. Some of the visitors fell in love with the islands and never left. Others came to trade and made many trips from the islands to other ports.

A sandalwood tree on the Big Island

China was a market hungry for Hawaiian **sandalwood**, which was used in medicines and as incense. European and American traders threw themselves into the sandalwood business beginning in the early 1790s. They persuaded chiefs to send commoners into the mountains to cut down sandalwood trees. They paid the chiefs with guns, cannons, rum, and other foreign goods.

The Hawaiians were very curious about the strange lands where the foreigners came from. Many adventurous young people left the islands to explore the world outside. Some settled in lands from China to Spain. The Europeans and Americans referred to these Hawaiian settlers as kanakas, or Native Hawaiians.

It is estimated that 300,000 to 400,000 people lived on the Hawaiian Islands at the time Captain Cook

FAQ

Q8 WHAT COUNTRIES DID THE VISITORS TO HAWAI'I COME FROM?

A8 Hawai'i had frequent visitors from Great Britain, France, Germany, China, and the United States. There were even voyagers from Alaska, which at that time was part of Russia!

WORD TO KNOW

sandalwood *heavy, sweet-smelling wood of a tree found in Hawai'i's mountains*

King Kamehameha I met Otto von Kotzebue, a Russian naval officer, and others in his expedition party in the early 1800s.

WORD TO KNOW

immunity *natural protection against disease*

arrived. The Hawaiians had never been exposed to European diseases such as smallpox, measles, and influenza. They had no natural **immunity** against these illnesses. Within 100 years, as many as 80 percent of the Native Hawaiians had died from these diseases.

THE KINGDOM OF HAWAI'I

Many of the foreigners who came to Hawai'i hoped to establish trading stations and colonies. Great Britain, France, and the United States all wanted to claim parts of the islands as their own.

When Captain Cook landed in Hawai'i, the islands were under four major chiefs and several lesser chieftains. Kamehameha I, chief of the Kohala district of the Big Island, wanted to be an ali'i nui (high or paramount chief) and decided to gather the islands under one rule.

In 1790, Kamehameha began to build a massive temple to the war god, Ku. The Puʻukohola Temple towered above the sea in Hawaiʻi's Kohala District. The dedication of the temple called for a human sacrifice. Kamehameha sacrificed his cousin Keoua, who had been his longtime rival.

By building the temple, Kamehameha was able to unite all of the districts of the island of Hawaiʻi under his rule. In 1796, he gained control of Kahoʻolawe, Oʻahu, Molokaʻi, Lānaʻi, and Maui. Finally, in 1810, Niʻihau and Kauaʻi joined Kamehameha's island empire, making him the sole ruler of the Kingdom of Hawaiʻi.

KAMEHAMEHA I: THE HARD-SHELLED CRAB

The Hawaiians had a nickname for King Kamehameha I (c. 1758–1819). They called him the Hard-Shelled Crab because of his strength and fearlessness in battle. A Russian sea captain wrote that he was "an unusual man gifted by nature with a great mind, a broad vision, and an unusually firm character." In 1810, Kamehameha united the islands and became their first king. He worked to keep Hawaiʻi a sovereign kingdom, yet open to new ideas from the outside world.

? Want to know more? See www.ksbe.edu/pauahi/history.php

Building the Puʻukohola Temple

SEE IT HERE!

THE NAHA STONE

On the lawn of the public library in the city of Hilo stands a great boulder, shaped roughly like a bench. According to a Hawaiian legend, the first chief who could lift this boulder, known as the Naha Stone, would unite the islands. Kamehameha I lifted the stone and went on to become the islands' first king!

42

King Kamehameha II was the second king of Hawai'i.

◄1819

Queen Ka'ahumanu helps brings an end to the kapu system

1820

The first Protestant missionaries arrive in Hawai'i

▲1830s

Whaling ships begin stopping at Hawaiian ports to take on supplies

CHAPTER FOUR

GROWTH AND CHANGE

★

AFTER THE DEATH OF KING KAMEHAMEHA I IN 1819, THE THRONE PASSED TO HIS SON LIHOLIHO. Liholiho became King Kamehameha II. He shared his rule with his kuhina nui, or prime minister, Queen Kaʻahumanu. She was one of the many widows of Kamehameha I. Kaʻahumanu was to make lasting changes in the Hawaiian way of life.

1860s ▶

Sugar becomes big business on the islands

1893

A group of planters overthrows Queen Liliʻuokalani

1898

Hawaiʻi becomes a possession of the United States

Queen Ka'ahumanu is credited with ending the kapu system.

THE BREAKING OF KAPU

Queen Ka'ahumanu was a determined, intelligent woman. She realized that the ancient kapu system was holding her back from achieving the more powerful positions in Hawaiian society. So she came up with a plan to end the kapu system.

Ka'ahumanu persuaded the weak new king to attend a special meal. Tables were set up at the royal palace. A group of women cooked fish and meat in the court imu. This was shocking behavior, because a strong kapu forbade women from cooking in the imu. Then the king broke one of the strictest kapu rules of all. He sat down with Ka'ahumanu and a group of other women and ate his meal with them! The guests at the feast stared in astonishment. Many were sure that the gods would bring down a terrible punishment. But the earth did not tremble, and fire did not rain from the sky. The king did not fall to the ground in agony. His actions showed that the rules of kapu could safely be broken.

News of the royal banquet flew from one island to the next. Within weeks, the Hawaiians threw the ancient kapu system aside. Chiefs and commoners smashed statues of the gods they had once feared and worshipped. Although some commoners and chiefs continued to worship the Hawaiian gods and goddesses, and chiefs continued to proclaim kapus, the ancient system of kapu was no longer the state religion.

MINI-BIO

KA'AHUMANU: THE KUHINA NUI

Ka'ahumanu (1768–1832) was the first and favorite wife of King Kamehameha I. In 1819, she became prime minister, or kuhina nui, under King Kamehameha II. Ka'ahumanu helped to end the ancient kapu system in the kingdom. Later, she converted to Christianity and encouraged the work of the Protestant missionaries who came to Hawai'i. She passed laws against stealing, murder, and smoking. Her last words reflected her Christian beliefs: "I'm going now, where the mansions are ready."

? Want to know more? See www.aloha-Hawaii.com/Hawaii/queen+kaahumanu

A MISSION TO SAVE SOULS

Early in 1819, a slim book became popular reading in New England. It told the story of a Hawaiian named Henry Opukaha'ia. He had left Hawai'i as a sailor and eventually arrived in New Haven, Connecticut. There, he **converted** to Christianity. According to the booklet, Opukaha'ia begged New England churches to send ministers to Hawai'i to bring the Christian faith to the people of the islands.

Henry Opukaha'ia never saw his island home again. He died in Connecticut at the age of 26. But his story filled many New Englanders with excitement. Churches raised money to send missionaries to

WORD TO KNOW

converted *changed*

A MISSIONARY HYMN

This hymn was written by a missionary seeking to change the ways of the Hawaiians' beliefs:

Soon may the heathen see the light,
Which dawns to close the pagan night,
And say with truth forever more,
Hawai'i's idols are no more.

Hawai'i. In 1820, a ship called the *Thaddeus* landed on the Big Island after a five-month voyage. The ship carried a group of Protestant ministers and their families. The leader of the group was a stern preacher named Hiram Bingham.

A crowd of barefoot Hawaiians rushed to the beach to greet the new arrivals. The missionaries were shocked to see Hawaiian women dressed in long skirts and nothing else. In dismay, Bingham wrote, "Can such beings be civilized? Can we throw ourselves upon these rude shores, [and live] among such a people for the purpose of training them for heaven?"

The missionaries met the king and the kuhina nui. Warily, Kamehameha II and Ka'ahumanu agreed to let them reside on the islands. The leaders were not much interested in a new religion, but felt that the mission-

Christian missionaries first settled in O'ahu in 1820. Here is a photograph of the site from the early 20th century.

aries could do no harm. Ka'ahumanu's feeling changed after she became seriously ill. Under the care of Sybil Bingham, the preacher's wife, she made a full recovery. Awed and grateful, she converted to Christianity. She urged the islanders to attend church and to adopt the religion of the foreigners.

One of the first tasks facing the missionaries was to translate the Bible into Hawaiian. But the Hawaiian language had no system of writing. Before they could translate the Bible, the missionaries had to devise a Hawaiian alphabet. Once this was done, they had to teach the Hawaiians to read and write.

Within a few years, the missionaries had opened schools on Hawai'i, O'ahu, and several other islands. By 1824, about 2,000 Hawaiian students were enrolled. That number zoomed to 52,000 by 1831. Almost two-fifths of the islanders were in school.

The Hawaiians enjoyed learning from the visiting missionaries. They turned it into a game and eagerly competed with one another. Reuben Tinker, a missionary in the port town of Honolulu, wrote that exam day was a kind of festival. "About 2,000 scholars were present," he recalled, "some wrapped in a large quantity of native cloth, with wreaths of evergreen about their heads and hanging toward their feet—others dressed in calico and silk with large necklaces of braided hair and wreaths of red and yellow and green feathers very beautiful and expensive."

Another task the missionaries set for themselves was to change the way Hawaiian women dressed. The wives of the missionaries designed long, loose-fitting dresses that covered the women from neck to ankles. The Hawaiian women soon came to accept the new clothing style.

FAQ

Q8 WHAT WAS THE ALPHABET THE MISSIONARIES INVENTED?

A8 The missionaries created an alphabet using 12 English letters: the five vowels plus the consonants h, k, l, m, n, p, and w. This writing system is still in use for the Hawaiian language.

Whalers capture a whale in the Pacific Ocean.

As more missionaries came to Hawai'i, they gained a strong influence in the government of the kingdom. They encouraged the Hawaiians to pass many new laws. One important change was the distribution of land. Until the 1840s, all of the land in the islands belonged to the king and the chiefs. The missionaries convinced King Kamehameha III (he succeeded his brother who died in 1824) to distribute about one-third of the land to the commoners. Many commoners were quickly persuaded to sell their land to Americans and Europeans.

RAISING CANE

During the 1830s, hundreds of American whaling ships began to sail the Pacific. Whaling was a big business. Whale oil was used as heating fuel and in lamps, where it gave a soft, steady light. Frequently, whalers stopped in the ports of Honolulu, Lahaina, and Hilo to take on supplies. Merchants in the ports sold food, rope, canvas, and other goods to the ships' captains. Taverns sprang up to cater to the sailors who came ashore. When a whaler was in port, the streets were loud with drunken singing and brawling. The missionaries protested, but there was little they could do. The whalers were a major source of income for the islands.

Within 30 years, the Pacific whales had nearly disappeared. By this time, a new business was flourishing in Hawai'i: the growing and **refining** of sugar. Westerners had begun experimenting with growing sugar in the mid-1820s. The first sugar plantation was established on Kaua'i in the mid-1830s. Most Hawaiian sugar was shipped to markets in California.

Raising and refining sugar called for many hands. The islands could not supply enough workers for the booming new industry. In the 1850s, the sugar planters began to import workers from China. Later, they brought workers from Tahiti, Japan, Portugal, and Germany. By 1886, the foreign population outnumbered the Native Hawaiians. They had become a minority in their own country.

WORD TO KNOW

refining *removing impurities; perfecting*

Q8 DID HAWAI'I EXPORT ANY OTHER CROPS BESIDES SUGAR?
A8 Hawai'i also exported oranges, mangoes, figs, and a fruit called the custard apple.

Workers harvesting sugarcane

'IOLANI PALACE

The name *'Iolani* comes from Hawaiian words meaning "royal hawk" and "of the heavens." King David Kalākaua hoped that 'Iolani Palace would restore the dignity of the Hawaiian royalty. When it was finished in 1882, the palace had the most modern conveniences of the time. Hawaiians marveled at its indoor plumbing, telephone system, and gas lighting. The palace also featured a throne room, state dining room, and Grand Hall, displaying many valuable paintings and statues from Europe and Asia.

WORD TO KNOW

monarch *king or queen*

The 'Iolani Palace a few years after its completion

THE MERRIE MONARCH

In 1874, U.S. president Ulysses S. Grant received a special guest at the White House. Hawai'i's newly crowned king, David Kalākaua, was given a royal welcome. King Kalākaua was the first **monarch** from any nation ever to visit the United States.

Kalākaua enjoyed fine clothes, rich food, and expensive works of art. Because he loved to host parties, he earned the nickname the Merrie Monarch. He had a serious side as well. He cared deeply about his country. He tried to preserve Native Hawaiian art, music, and storytelling.

In 1881, Kalākaua ordered the building of a magnificent new royal palace in Honolulu. When the 'Iolani Palace was completed in 1882, he had himself crowned in a lavish ceremony. The costs of the palace and the coronation were immense. As a result, King Kalākaua led his nation into deep debt.

American sugar planters and other businessmen were hungry to gain more power in the Hawaiian government. In 1887, they pressured the debt-ridden government to accept a new constitution. Under the Bayonet Constitution, as it came to be called, only property owners could vote. Despite the fact that a powerful queen had once helped rule the land, women—as well as Native Hawaiians, Chinese, Japanese, and Filipino people—were not allowed to vote for quite some time. This rule gave greater power to the planters and took voting rights away from most Native Hawaiians. The constitution also made Honolulu's Pearl Harbor an American naval base.

THE PRISONER QUEEN

When King Kalākaua died in 1891, the throne passed to his sister, Princess Liliʻuokalani. Queen Liliʻuokalani was strong and determined. She was the only reigning queen in the history of Hawaiʻi. She knew that the Americans wanted to turn Hawaiʻi into a territory of the United States. She decided to fight for her country's independence. For two years, she gathered support and made careful plans. In January 1893, she announced that the Bayonet Constitution would be set aside. She intended to restore the Constitution of 1864, returning the vote to all Hawaiian citizens, including women.

Alarmed at losing power, a group of American planters and businessmen decided to take matters into their own hands. They hastily formed an organization called the Committee of Safety. They chose lawyer Sanford Dole, the son of missionaries, to head a temporary new government. A band of U.S. Marines stationed in Honolulu rushed to help. In a bloodless takeover, the Committee of Safety placed the queen

King Kalākaua was the first ruler of any country to make a trip around the world. On a worldwide tour in 1881, he visited many countries including China, Japan, India, Burma, several European nations, and the United States.

EMMA AIMA NAWAHI: HAWAIIAN PATRIOT, WOMEN'S SUFFRAGIST, AND JOURNALIST

Emma Aima Nawahi (1854–1934) was born in Hilo, on the Big Island of Hawai'i. She grew up with a strong sense of Hawaiian tradition and culture, and quickly became one of Queen Lili'uokalani's advisers. When Lili'uokalani and the Hawaiian government were overthrown in 1893, Nawahi began a campaign to fight against the "New Republic of Hawai'i." She and her husband, Joseph, founded *Ke Aloha Aina (The Patriot)* newspaper in 1895, to promote the return of Hawaiian sovereignty. She continued to work as an editor for the newspaper, advocating for women's voting rights, until 1920, when the 19th Amendment granted women the right to vote.

? Want to know more? See www.museumoftheamericanwest.org/explore/exhibits/suffrage/nawahi_full.html

under house arrest in 'Iolani Palace. The American flag now flew over the post office in Honolulu.

The Committee of Safety sent word of the queen's overthrow to the U.S. government in Washington. It urged the United States to annex Hawai'i at once. President Grover Cleveland was horrified when he learned what had happened. He refused to annex Hawai'i. The Hawaiian monarchy was never restored, however. For five years, Hawai'i was a republic, with Sanford Dole as its president. The queen remained a prisoner.

In 1898, the United States fought a brief war with Spain. Much of the fighting took place in the Pacific, around the Spanish-held Philippine Islands. The United States wanted a military base in the Pacific. By this time, a new president, William McKinley, was in the White House. McKinley was prepared to annex Hawai'i.

On August 12, 1898, spectators crowded into 'Iolani Palace. They had gathered to watch the ceremony that would make Hawai'i a possession of the United States. A band played the Hawaiian national anthem for the last time. Slowly, the Hawaiian flag was lowered on its staff. As the flag slid toward the ground, a burst

The Hawaiian flag was lowered and removed from outside 'Iolani Palace on August 12, 1898.

of wailing broke the solemn moment. At a nearby church, a group of Hawaiian women chanted the traditional song of mourning. Their voices of grief made a grim background as the U.S. flag caught the wind to fly above the palace walls. Hawaiians had no say as their country passed to foreign hands.

READ ABOUT

The U.S.
possession of
Hawai'i was
marked by a
ceremony at 'Iolani
Palace on August
12, 1898.

1900

*Hawai'i becomes
a U.S. territory*

1941 ▲

*Japanese bombers attack
Pearl Harbor, bringing the
United States into World War
II; Hawai'i is placed under
martial law*

1942

*The U.S. Army forms
the 100th Battalion
with Japanese
American soldiers*

CHAPTER FIVE

MORE MODERN TIMES

★

IN 1900, HAWAI'I BECAME A U.S. TERRITORY. Some citizens in Hawai'i hoped that becoming a territory would be a step toward statehood. Though the territory soon became a popular destination for U.S. travelers, many decades and many changes lay ahead before statehood became a reality.

▲1993

President Bill Clinton signs a resolution apologizing for the U.S. overthrow of the Kingdom of Hawai'i

2007

The Pu'uhonua o Honaunau National Historical Park expands to preserve the remains of an ancient coastal village

1959 ▲

Hawai'i becomes the 50th state

BECOMING AN AMERICAN

Under the U.S. Constitution today, any foreign-born person in the United States may become an American citizen if he or she meets certain requirements. In 1900, however, native-born Chinese and Japanese persons did not have this right. Many Americans felt that Asian cultures were too different from the culture of the United States. They feared that Asians would never fit in and would cause problems. Asians were not allowed to apply for U.S. citizenship until 1952.

Japanese workers made up the largest portion of the sugar plantation labor force.

Q8 WHO WAS HAWAI'I'S FIRST TERRITORIAL GOVERNOR?

A8 President Theodore Roosevelt appointed Sanford Dole to be the first territorial governor of Hawai'i, in 1900.

THE TERRITORY OF HAWAI'I

When Hawai'i became a U.S. territory, many Hawaiians automatically became U.S. citizens. However, citizenship did not extend to Hawaiians born in China or Japan. Laws in the United States prevented Asians from applying for citizenship.

As a territory, Hawai'i could send one delegate to the U.S. Congress. The territorial delegate could speak in Congress but did not have the right to vote. Hawaiians could not vote in presidential elections, yet the U.S. president appointed the territorial governor.

Hawai'i first applied to become a state in 1903, but Congress turned down the request. Hawai'i applied over and over in the years that followed. Again and again, the request was denied. Congress felt that Hawai'i's large Asian population made it too foreign to be a state—even though the legislators' own ancestors were foreign-born.

THE BIG FIVE

During the early 1900s, five companies gained control of Hawai'i's plantations. Much like the chiefs of long ago, these powerful companies ran the government of the islands. Americans owned four of the "Big Five," and the fifth company was owned by Germans.

At first, 90 percent of Hawai'i's income came from sugar. Then James Dole, Governor Sanford Dole's cousin, invested in pineapples. Pineapples were first planted in Hawai'i during the 1880s, but few people thought that this odd, prickly fruit could make money. James Dole proved them wrong. Soon pineapples were Hawai'i's second most valuable crop.

About 60 percent of Hawai'i's plantation workers came from Japan. In the early 1900s, the planters continued searching for other sources of cheap labor. They brought in workers from Puerto Rico and the Philippines. They also hired some African Americans from Tennessee. The Japanese workers generally earned the lowest pay, as little as 69 cents an hour. Portuguese laborers were paid $1.50 an hour for the same work.

In protest, a group of Japanese workers on O'ahu formed an organization called the Higher Wages Association (HWA). In 1909, the HWA led a strike of 7,000 Japanese sugarcane workers. The strikers demanded better working conditions and a pay raise to $1 an hour. The planters fought back brutally. About 5,000 strikers and their families were driven from their homes. After three months, the strike was broken and the Japanese went back to work for the same low wages.

THE EARTHLY PARADISE

In 1890, a pamphlet called the *Hawai'i Guide Book* was being sold in the United States. It was filled with

SEE IT HERE!

KEOMUKU VILLAGE

In 1898, Keomuku Village was built as a sugar plantation on the island of Lāna'i. The plantation was abandoned in 1901 when the drinking water turned salty. Today, Keomuku is a ghost town. You can still see some of the workers' cabins and the mill where sugar was once processed.

In 1922, James Dole bought the whole island of Lāna'i to be his private pineapple plantation. He paid $1.1 million. The very next year, he cleared a profit of almost $2.8 million!

MINI-BIO

FRED KINZABURO MAKINO: A VOICE FOR THE UNDERDOG

In 1909, Fred Kinzaburo Makino (1877–1953) helped lead a strike of Japanese sugarcane workers on O'ahu. Three years later, he founded a Japanese-language newspaper. His paper, the *Hawai'i Hochi* (*Hawai'i News*) was published for the next 80 years. It strongly supported the rights of Hawai'i's Japanese population, and called for the right of citizenship for these inhabitants.

 Want to know more? See http://clear.uhwo.hawaii.edu/LaborBios.html

descriptions of gorgeous sunsets, stunning mountains, and clean, sparkling beaches. "The Earthly Paradise!" the book began. "Don't you want to go to it? Why of course."

By the last days of the Kingdom of Hawai'i, visitors began to make their way to the islands. Hawai'i's natural beauty was all they had hoped for. But Hawai'i had no nightclubs, fancy hotels, or fine restaurants. In the early 1900s, business owners set about to change this situation. They opened grand hotels in Honolulu and nearby Waikīkī. Swampland around Waikīkī was cleared to make the beach more attractive to bathers. The Hawai'i Visitors Bureau worked to promote tourism. It encouraged the development of tourist attractions and spread the word about Hawai'i to people on the U.S. mainland. More and more tourists arrived in Hawai'i. By 1931, the number of visitors reached 16,000 in a single year.

WAR AND HARD TIMES

In December 1912, a U.S. naval ship, the USS *California*, steamed into Pearl Harbor. Two famous Hawaiians—former governor Sanford Dole and former queen Lili'uokalani—climbed aboard for a welcome ceremony. This was the first time the two had come face-to-face since the Committee of Safety overthrew the monarchy in 1893.

Since 1901, Pearl Harbor had been deepened and widened to hold large seagoing ships. The *California*

A U.S. submarine travels through Pearl Harbor in the 1920s.

was the first large naval vessel to dock there. In the following years, Pearl Harbor served as an important fueling station for the U.S. Navy. In the early 1900s, steamships were powered by coal. But they could not carry enough coal for a voyage across the Pacific. Ships stopped at Pearl Harbor, took on a fresh coal supply, and steamed on their way.

In 1917, the United States was swept into World War I. As the United States fought Germany, anti-German feeling swelled in Hawai'i, despite German American citizens who remained patriotic to America. German language classes were dropped from schools. Teachers of German heritage were fired. A group of Germans from a stranded merchant ship were forced to work on plantations on Maui until the end of the war. One of the Big Five, the German-owned company H. Hackfeld, was seized and sold to American investors.

During the 1930s, the world slid into a disastrous economic depression. Factories closed, farm prices fell, and millions of people lost their jobs. The Great Depression hit hard in Hawai'i. A 1932 report claimed that 10 per-

Smoke fills the sky during the December 7, 1941, attack on Pearl Harbor.

cent of the workforce in Honolulu was unemployed. No one knew the figures for other places in Hawai'i.

The prices for sugar and pineapples tumbled. Field workers lost their jobs or were put on shortened shifts. The territorial government tried to ease unemployment by sending away foreign workers. In 1932 and 1933, about 10,000 Filipino laborers were sent back to their homeland. Planters were urged to hire unemployed Hawaiians rather than foreign workers.

By the late 1930s, the Depression began to ease. In Hawai'i, one area especially brought jobs and income: the military. Work continued at Pearl Harbor. O'ahu's Hickam and Wheeler airfields expanded. Troops poured into Schofield Army Base. The United States was getting ready for war.

BOMBERS OVER PEARL HARBOR

On the morning of December 7, 1941, the people of Honolulu heard the roar of airplanes overhead. Most thought that U.S. aircraft were practicing maneuvers. Then the terrifying thunder of explosions ripped the air. A

FAQ

Q8 HOW MANY PEOPLE WERE KILLED IN THE ATTACK ON PEARL HARBOR?

A8 The attack took the lives of 2,390 U.S. military personnel and 57 civilians. Sixty-four Japanese are known to have died.

radio announcer declared, "This is no test. This is the real McCoy. Pearl Harbor is being bombed by the Japanese."

For nearly a year, the United States and Japan had been preparing for war. The U.S. government knew that military bases on Hawai'i might be a target. Nevertheless, the Japanese raid on December 7 took everyone by surprise. For close to two hours, Japanese bombs pounded the U.S. Pacific Fleet stationed at Pearl Harbor. The attack destroyed 21 naval vessels, about one-third of the entire U.S. fleet.

As the Japanese planes zoomed away, Hawai'i's governor, Joseph Poindexter, handed over his power to U.S. Army general Walter Short. Hawai'i was under **martial law**. Short stated that martial law would be lifted as soon as the danger of another attack had passed. The military remained in charge of Hawai'i for the next three years.

Under martial law, the military had control over life in the islands. It set prices for food and other goods. Mail, newspapers, and radio broadcasts were censored. Anyone could be arrested without charge and kept in jail for as long as the military saw fit.

On December 8, 1941, President Franklin D. Roosevelt declared war on Japan. Three days later, German dictator Adolf

WORD TO KNOW

martial law *military law, military control*

MINI-BIO

DORIS "DORIE" MILLER: THE HERO OF PEARL HARBOR

During World War II, racial segregation was a fact of life in the U.S. Navy. When Doris "Dorie" Miller (1919–1943) enlisted, he and other African Americans were not allowed to train for combat duty. Miller was assigned to work as a food server on the USS Arizona, one of the battleships stationed at Pearl Harbor. When the Japanese attacked, however, he rushed to help his crewmates fire on the enemy planes. For his heroism, he was awarded the Navy Cross, the navy's second-highest honor. He died two years later when his ship, the USS Liscome Bay, was sunk by a torpedo from a Japanese submarine off the Pacific island of Butaritari. In his honor, the U.S. Navy in 1973 commissioned a new frigate— the USS Miller.

 Want to know more? See www.history.navy.mil/faqs/faq57-4.htm

Hitler declared war against the United States. The United States fought World War II on two fronts, in Europe and in the Pacific.

About one-third of all Hawaiians were of Japanese ancestry. Many haoles (foreign-born residents) doubted that the Japanese were loyal to the United States. Rumors of their spying flew among the islands.

Some hysterical voices demanded that all the Japanese people in Hawai'i be locked in prison camps. On the U.S. mainland, about 110,000 Japanese Americans were sent to special camps during the war. Few Japanese in Hawai'i, however, were imprisoned. Japanese labor was too important in the islands. Without Japanese hands, the islands' industries would come to a standstill.

Early in 1942, a group of Japanese college students wrote a letter to the military governor. They explained, "Hawai'i is our home, the United States is our country. . . . We wish to do our part as loyal Americans in every way possible and we hereby offer ourselves for whatever service you may see fit to use us."

The U.S. Army accepted these eager young Japanese Americans. They formed the 100th Battalion, which was sent to fight in Europe. In 1943, Japanese troops from

THE USS ARIZONA NATIONAL MEMORIAL

One of the 21 ships that sank on December 7, 1941, was the USS *Arizona*. Today, those who died are honored at the USS *Arizona* National Memorial. The memorial spans the sunken hull of the ship like a bridge. At the entrance, visitors see one of the ship's original bells. Flying above the monument, the U.S. flag is attached to the mast of the sunken battleship. The names of the 1,177 people who died on the *Arizona* are engraved on the marble wall of the memorial's Shrine Room.

The memorial was dedicated in 1962. Both American and Japanese visitors come each year to pay their respects to the dead. Every day, about 2 quarts (1.8 liters) of the ship's oil slowly leaks to the surface. This leaking oil is called "the tears of the *Arizona*."

USS *Arizona*
National Memorial

Hawai'i: From Territory to Statehood (1900–1959)

This map shows the area that became the state of Hawai'i in 1959.

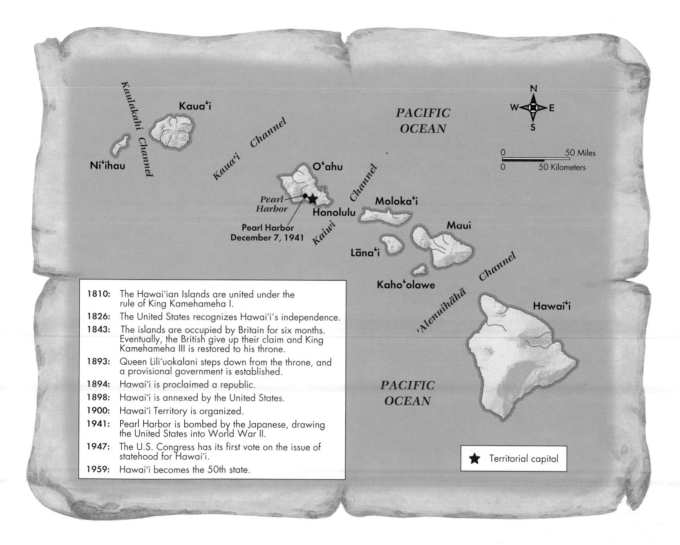

PACIFIC OCEAN

Kaua'i

Ni'ihau

Kaulakahi Channel

Kaua'i Channel

O'ahu

Pearl Harbor

Honolulu

Pearl Harbor
December 7, 1941

Moloka'i

Kaiwi Channel

Lāna'i

Kaho'olawe

Maui

'Alenuihāhā Channel

Hawai'i

PACIFIC OCEAN

1810: The Hawai'ian Islands are united under the rule of King Kamehameha I.

1826: The United States recognizes Hawai'i's independence.

1843: The islands are occupied by Britain for six months. Eventually, the British give up their claim and King Kamehameha III is restored to his throne.

1893: Queen Lili'uokalani steps down from the throne, and a provisional government is established.

1894: Hawai'i is proclaimed a republic.

1898: Hawai'i is annexed by the United States.

1900: Hawai'i Territory is organized.

1941: Pearl Harbor is bombed by the Japanese, drawing the United States into World War II.

1947: The U.S. Congress has its first vote on the issue of statehood for Hawai'i.

1959: Hawai'i becomes the 50th state.

★ Territorial capital

the mainland were added. The unit became the 100th Battalion-442nd Infantry. The 100th-442nd was known for its bravery under fire. For its size, it was the most highly decorated unit of the war.

THE ROAD TO STATEHOOD

During the war years (1941–1945), U.S. soldiers and sailors poured into Hawai'i. The population of the territory nearly doubled. These young men and women enjoyed the gentle climate, glorious scenery, and friendly warmth of the Hawaiian people. After the war, they carried home stories of the great times they had spent in the islands. To Americans on the mainland, Hawai'i began to seem less strange and forbidding.

After World War II, leaders in Hawai'i again applied to the U.S. Congress for statehood. Again, several applications were denied. Then at last, in the summer of 1959, the territories of Alaska and Hawai'i were both admitted into the Union. On August 21, 1959, Hawai'i became the 50th American state.

Hawai'i's first elections showed the state's racial diversity. The first governor was a haole, William F. Quinn. His lieutenant governor was James K. Kealoha, a Native Hawaiian. One of Hawai'i's first U.S. senators was a man of Chinese descent, Hiram L. Fong. A Japanese American veteran of the 100th-442nd, Daniel K. Inouye, became the state's first representative in Congress.

A newspaper headline announces Hawai'i's statehood.

ALOHA ʻĀINA

In the years after statehood, Hawaiʻi saw a tremendous construction boom. On Oʻahu, bulldozers roared and mighty cranes sprang up like weeds. Highways tunneled beneath the mountains. Dozens of gleaming new office buildings opened in Honolulu. Luxury hotels soared above Waikiki and other beaches. On Maui, Kauaʻi, and Hawaiʻi, building got under way as well.

Tourists flocked to Hawaiʻi from the United States, Canada, Japan, Hong Kong, and Singapore. They were drawn to the dazzling beauty of the islands. Yet the increase in tourism and construction threatened its natural splendor.

During the 1970s, Hawaiians from every ethnic group worked together to protect the environment. Their motto was aloha ʻāina, or "love of the land." The concept of aloha ʻāina was part of Native Hawaiian life before the arrival of the Europeans.

The plight of the island of Kahoʻolawe troubled many people who cared about the environment. Kahoʻolawe had been under military control since 1941.

THINK ABOUT IT!

The Price of Tourism

Tourism is the biggest industry in Hawaiʻi today. How can millions of people visit the islands each year without polluting the air, water, and land? Can tourism respect the Native Hawaiian values of aloha ʻāina? "In putting the guest first, the place and good will of the host are sacrificed," said Dennis Kanahele, a descendant of King Kamehameha I. "It is important to preserve the dignity and cultural landscape of the place."

The U.S. Navy and Marine Corps used it as a target for bombing practice. After decades of bombing, the island was nearly a lifeless wasteland. Environmentalists wanted to see it restored as a nature preserve and cultural center. In 1976, protesters began to visit the island, demanding that it be returned to the state of Hawai'i. Several protesters were arrested and sent to prison. At last, in 1994, President Bill Clinton returned Kaho'olawe to the people of Hawai'i.

THE QUESTION OF INDEPENDENCE

On November 23, 1993, President Bill Clinton signed the Apology Resolution. On behalf of the American people, Clinton apologized for the overthrow of Queen Lili'uokalani and the Hawaiian monarchy. The Apology Resolution was an open admission that the United States had been wrong to take over the Hawaiian kingdom.

Some Hawaiians saw the Apology Resolution as a step toward independence for the islands. The Hawaiian independence movement had been gathering strength since the 1980s. One of its leaders was a Honolulu lawyer named Mililani Trask. After years of effort in the Native Hawaiian community, she founded Ka Lahui, or the Nation of Hawai'i. The Nation of Hawai'i sought to restore the Hawaiian monarchy. It hoped to make Hawai'i a **sovereign** nation.

Only a small group of people in Hawai'i wanted complete independence from the United States. Many more supported the idea of giving Native Hawaiians special rights to the land. They believed that Native Hawaiians deserved help from the government because they lost so much with the U.S. takeover.

Not everyone agreed, however. Lawyer H. William Burgess and his wife, Sandra Puanani Burgess, insisted

WORD TO KNOW

sovereign *independent, under its own government*

Visitors explore Pu'uhonua o Honaunau
National Historical Park

that no group should have more privileges than any other. "We believe in advocating for aloha for all," explained Sandra Burgess, who is part Native Hawaiian. "It means that all citizens, whatever their ancestry, are entitled to equal protection under the law."

In 2007, the people of Hawai'i celebrated the end of a 30-year effort to expand Pu'uhonua o Honaunau National Historical Park on the island of Hawai'i. The park now includes the remains of an ancient fishing village that may be 1,000 years old. "This site is of great significance to Native Hawaiians, students of history and archaeology, and the people of Hawai'i today," said Senator Daniel Akaka at the dedication ceremony. "This land can now be celebrated by the wider public."

In the 21st century, Hawai'i continues to develop tourism and other industries. Yet the people of Hawai'i honor their past as they look with hope toward their future.

READ ABOUT

Hula dancers perform, celebrating traditional Hawaiian culture and welcoming visitors to the islands.

CHAPTER SIX

PEOPLE

★

A BOATBUILDER HOLDS A CEREMONY TO CHRISTEN HIS NEWEST YACHT. A fifth-grade class raises money to help protect endangered monk seals. A restaurant manager posts a sign announcing the day's specials. Whatever their daily business might be, Hawaiians are very friendly people. Hawaiʻi's nickname is the Aloha State. Hawaiians extend their aloha spirit of welcome and warmth to loved ones, neighbors, and strangers.

Students in the city of Lāna'i

One of every five Hawaiians describes himself or herself as belonging to two or more races!

MEET THE HAWAIIANS

According to the 2006 estimates, 1,285,498 people live in Hawai'i, putting it in 42nd place in population among the states. Despite its small size, Hawai'i is the most ethnically diverse state in the nation. People from every part of the globe have chosen to make Hawai'i their home. Today, no single ethnic group makes up as much as 50 percent of the population.

Where Hawaiians Live

The colors on this map indicate population density throughout the state. The darker the color, the more people live there.

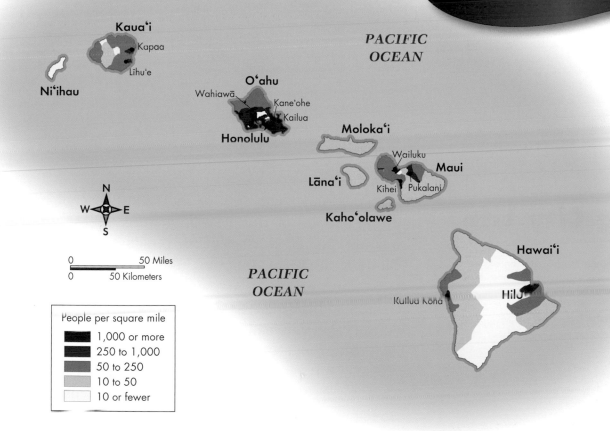

Kaua'i
Kapaa
Lihu'e
Ni'ihau

PACIFIC OCEAN

O'ahu
Wahiawā
Kane'ohe
Kailua
Honolulu

Moloka'i
Wailuku
Maui
Lāna'i
Kihei
Pukalani
Kaho'olawe

PACIFIC OCEAN

N
W   E
S

0   50 Miles
0   50 Kilometers

Hawai'i
Kailua Kona
Hilo

People per square mile

■	1,000 or more
■	250 to 1,000
■	50 to 250
■	10 to 50
☐	10 or fewer

People QuickFacts

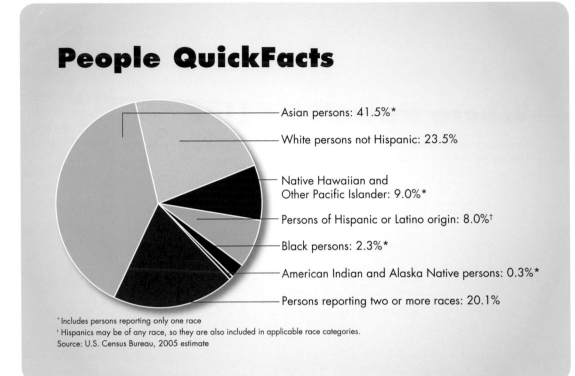

Asian persons: 41.5%*

White persons not Hispanic: 23.5%

Native Hawaiian and
Other Pacific Islander: 9.0%*

Persons of Hispanic or Latino origin: 8.0%†

Black persons: 2.3%*

American Indian and Alaska Native persons: 0.3%*

Persons reporting two or more races: 20.1%

* Includes persons reporting only one race
† Hispanics may be of any race, so they are also included in applicable race categories.
Source: U.S. Census Bureau, 2005 estimate

Big City Life

This shows the population of Hawai'i's only city with a population of more than 100,000 people.

Honolulu   377,357

Source: U.S. Census Bureau, 2006 estimates

People of Asian and Pacific Island descent make up 50 percent of Hawai'i's population. These groups include people whose backgrounds are Japanese, Chinese, Korean, Filipino, Polynesian, or Native Hawaiian. About 24 percent of all Hawaiians are Caucasian (or haoles, as they are called in the islands). Hawai'i also has small populations of Hispanics, African Americans, and Native Americans.

About 91 percent of Hawaiians are urban dwellers. This means they live in cities or large towns. About three-quarters of all Hawaiians live on O'ahu. Honolulu, on O'ahu, is the only city in Hawai'i with more than 100,000 people.

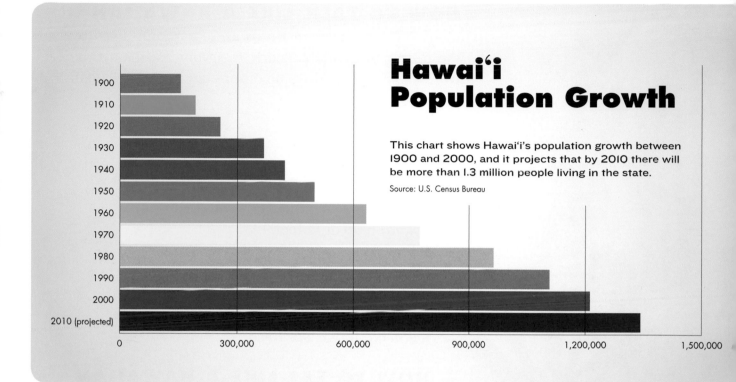

Hawai'i Population Growth

This chart shows Hawai'i's population growth between 1900 and 2000, and it projects that by 2010 there will be more than 1.3 million people living in the state.

Source: U.S. Census Bureau

THE HAWAIIAN LANGUAGE

Few people today speak Hawaiian as their first language. However, many people use a blend of languages known as **Pidgin**. Pidgin in Hawai'i is a spicy stew of words from Hawaiian, English, Japanese, Chinese, Filipino Tagalog, and other languages.

One person who is trying to promote Pidgin is Lee Tonouchi. As a student at the University of Hawai'i, he insisted on writing his term papers in Pidgin. Today, he writes poetry, plays, and short stories in Pidgin, and he speaks in Pidgin when he appears on talk shows. Tonouchi has been nicknamed the Pidgin Guerrilla because he fights to have Pidgin taken seriously.

Q IS HAWAIIAN STILL SPOKEN ANYWHERE IN THE ISLANDS?

A Hawaiian is still the first language of many people on the island of Ni'ihau.

WORD TO KNOW

Pidgin *a language consisting of words and grammar from two or more languages*

A lei

HOW TO TALK LIKE A HAWAIIAN

Many Native Hawaiian words are commonly used by the people of Hawai'i. Nearly everyone has heard the word *aloha*. Here are some other Hawaiian words you may not know.

kane: boy or man

wahine: girl or woman

pau: finished (with a meal or task)

pau hana: the end of the workday or school day

kama'aina: longtime resident of Hawai'i

kokua: help or helper

lei: necklace of shells or flowers

luau: feast

makai: in the direction of the sea

mauka: in the direction of the mountains

wikiwiki: quick, speedy

HOW TO EAT LIKE A HAWAIIAN

No party is complete without great food. This is especially true in Hawai'i! A luau is a Hawaiian feast. At a luau, you may taste flavors from around the world—from China, Japan, Samoa, Portugal, and many other countries. Hawai'i also has its own traditional foods. Most come from the sea or from the delicious fruits and vegetables that grow on the islands. Check out the menu on the opposite page for a sampling of luau foods that are chiefly of Hawaiian origin.

Fruit at a luau

MENU

WHAT'S ON THE MENU IN HAWAI'I?

★ ★ ★

Fresh Pineapple

Pineapple can be eaten alone, in fruit salads, or in desserts.

Lau lau

This appetizer is made from fish or chicken, wrapped in taro leaves, and steamed.

Kalua pig

This is a pig that is slow-cooked in a Hawaiian imu or pit oven. It is the centerpiece of a traditional luau.

Mango bread

Delicious bread flavored with mashed mango.

Poi

This thick pasty side dish is made from pounded taro and can be scooped up with the fingers. Poi is described as "one-finger," "two-finger," or "three-finger," depending on its thickness.

TRY THIS RECIPE
Haupia

This Hawaiian coconut pudding is a favorite dessert in the islands. Give it a try, but be sure to have an adult nearby to help.

Ingredients:
2 cups coconut milk
6 tablespoons sugar
5 tablespoons cornstarch
1 cup whole milk

Instructions:
Pour 1 cup of the coconut milk into a saucepan. In a separate bowl, mix the sugar and cornstarch. Add this mixture to the coconut milk in the saucepan. Stir over low heat. Slowly add the rest of the coconut milk and the whole milk. The mixture will thicken as you stir. Serve it warm or chilled.

Haupia topped with fruit

HAWAIIAN ART, PAST AND PRESENT

Before the arrival of the Europeans, Native Hawaiian artists and craftspeople used the materials they found around them. From the feathers of wild birds, they wove amazing cloaks and banners for their chiefs. They decorated kapa fabric with complex designs. Island sculptors carved wooden figures of gods and goddesses to be honored in the temples. Even the handles of tools and spears were carved with figures of gods.

Another traditional art form in Hawai'i is the lei. A lei is a necklace made of flowers, small fruits, colorful seeds, or tiny shells. Each island has developed its own style of lei-making. For example, the people of Ni'ihau use shells, and Kaua'i is known for leis made from a small, fragrant fruit called the mokihana. Leis from Moloka'i are made from the flowers of the candlenut tree.

At festivals and ceremonies, the Hawaiians perform a dance called the hula. The hula is accompanied by chants and drums. Through gestures and body motions, the dancers tell a story in pantomime.

The early missionaries from New England worked hard to stamp out most traditional Hawaiian art forms. They convinced the Hawaiians that dancing the hula was sinful. They destroyed carvings of gods and goddesses, and encouraged the Hawaiians to wear European-style clothing. Within a few decades, the Native Hawaiians had nearly forgotten their ancient traditions.

King David Kalākaua and Queen Lili'uokalani wanted Hawaiians to

take pride in their culture. They sparked a revival of hula, carving, and traditional Hawaiian music. During the 20th century, new kinds of art and music flooded into Hawai'i from all over the world. Modern and ancient art forms melded together, resulting in unique new forms.

ART AND ARTISTS

Hawai'i is one of the most beautiful places on Earth. Not surprisingly, it is an inspiration to painters and sculptors. Many of Hawai'i's artists bring a unique, modern approach to ancient traditions.

Like the Hawaiian carvers of old, Michael Lee fashions exquisite sculptures from the wood of native trees. Most of his subjects come from the natural world. Lee's carvings include animals, shells, and bird's nests.

A very different artist is Christopher Reiner, who turns discarded appliances into furniture. One of his pieces, *Vanidiere*, is a vanity chest made from a 1956 refrigerator. Reiner hopes that his work will make people more aware of waste in modern society. He

SEE IT HERE!

DOLPHINS OF MAKAPU'U POINT

On a wall at Sea Life Park in Waimanalo, O'ahu, is a **mural** entitled *Dolphins of Makapu'u Point*. The painter, Robert Wyland (1956–), grew up in Michigan but now makes O'ahu his home. Wyland's murals of ocean mammals can be seen all over the world. Because many of his murals feature whales, he calls them "whaling walls." Wyland plans to complete 100 whaling walls by 2010.

WORD TO KNOW

mural *painting on a wall*

Michael Lee used gold and several types of wood in his sculpture *On the Beach*.

HERB KAWAINUI KANE: PICTURING HISTORY

The paintings of Herb Kawainui Kane (1928–) reflect his fascination with Hawaiian history and culture. When he was growing up, his family moved several times, first from Waipio Valley to Hilo and later to Wisconsin. Kane studied art at the Art Institute of Chicago and then returned to Hawai'i. Among his books are *Pele: Goddess of Hawai'i's Volcanoes* (1987), *Voyagers* (1991), and *Ancient Hawai'i* (1998). In 1975, Kane designed and served as captain on the sailing canoe *Hokule'a*. Built in the style of the ancient Polynesian voyaging canoes, the *Hokule'a* made five round-trip journeys from Hawai'i to Polynesia, all without modern instruments!

Want to know more? See www.herbkaneart.com

Herb Kawainui Kane painting *The Cook Expedition Entering Kealakekua Bay, January 1779*

explains, "I just think people should think about what they throw away and try to be more creative in finding other ways to use things."

WRITING ABOUT HAWAI'I

The missionaries who came to Hawai'i in the 1820s and 1830s kept busy building schools and converting natives. But somehow many of them also found time to write about their experiences. Female missionaries were especially devoted to writing. Laura Fish Judd (1804–1872) and Charlotte Fowler Baldwin (1805–1873) both kept detailed journals about their experiences. Judd also wrote a book about early Honolulu.

Many famous writers have visited Hawai'i and written about their impressions. Most were dazzled by the beauty of the islands and intrigued by the blend of cultures. Mark Twain (1837–1910) is best known for books such as *The Adventures of Huckleberry Finn* and *Life on the Mississippi*. He traveled widely beyond his native Missouri and described some of his adventures in a book called *Roughing It*. In that book, he wrote about his experiences on Maui, O'ahu, and the Big Island during a visit in 1866.

Jack London is usually remembered for his tales about life in the Arctic. Yet Hawai'i was the setting for several of London's short stories. He paid the islands a long visit in 1907.

In 1960, a year after Hawai'i became a state, James Michener's massive novel *Hawai'i* soared to the bestseller list. Michener told the story of the islands from their volcanic formation to the days of modern tourism. Although it is a work of fiction, the novel brings Hawai'i's history fully to life.

Lois Lowry, who was born in Honolulu, is a young adult author who is well known for her *Anastasia* series. She won a Newbery Medal in 1993 for *The Giver*.

MUSIC AND DANCE

Hula underwent a revival with the help of King Kalākaua and Queen Lili'uokalani. The few dancers who had kept the tradi-

GRAHAM SALISBURY: YOUNG ADULT AUTHOR

Graham Salisbury (1944—) has a way of making the Hawaiian landscape come to life. Raised in Hawai'i, he has set many of his novels for young adults, including *Under the Blood-Red Sun*, *Shark Bait*, and *Jungle Dogs*, in Hawai'i. Salisbury's first novel, *Blue Skin of the Sea*, tells of his own childhood on the islands. He has won several awards for his work, among them an American Library Association Best Book for Young Adults award for *Under the Blood-Red Sun*.

? **Want to know more?** See www.grahamsalisbury.com

Lois Lowry

MINI-BIO

HELEN KAPUAILOHIA DESHA BEAMER: HAWAIIAN COMPOSER AND HULA TEACHER

When Helen Kapuailohia Desha Beamer (1882–1952) was growing up on the island of Oʻahu, her mother taught her the traditional chants of the hula. Beamer went on to teach many students the hula and Hawaiian poetry set to her own musical compositions to accompany them. Her efforts, and those of her peers, helped to preserve and perpetuate the illustrious culture of ancient and modern Hawaii to the dismay of overzealous missionaries.

? Want to know more? See www. hawaiimusicmuseum.org/honorees/1995/beamer.html

FAQ

Q8 HOW DID THE UKULELE GET TO HAWAIʻI?

A8 Portuguese immigrants brought the ukulele to Hawaiʻi in 1879. The instrument was originally called the braga.

A ukulele

tion alive were eager to teach new students. By the 1920s, hula dancers were admired around the world. Modern hula still tells stories through movement. It is usually accompanied by stringed instruments such as the guitar or ukulele. In Hawaiʻi, school-age children study hula much as children in other states take ballet or tap lessons.

During the early 19th century, sailors from whaling ships brought the guitar to Hawaiʻi. The Hawaiians quickly developed their own style of playing. By loosening the strings, they made the notes slide up and down in new ways. Today, the "slide guitar" belongs to the modern style of Hawaiian music.

Another instrument with a strong Hawaiian connection is the ukulele. The ukulele has four strings and resembles a small guitar. It became popular in Hawaiʻi during the 1920s and 1930s. The name ukulele comes from Hawaiian words meaning "jumping flea." According to legend, an English army officer named Edward Purvis was one of the first people in Hawaiʻi to master the instrument. The Hawaiians nicknamed him Jumping Flea when they saw how his fingers leaped and darted over the strings. The name eventually passed from Purvis to the instrument itself.

SPORTS

When Captain Cook and his crew reached Hawai'i in 1778, they were astonished to see Hawaiians riding the waves on long, wooden planks. Surfing is the most ancient American sport. It probably came to Hawai'i from Polynesia hundreds of years before Europeans arrived. The Hawaiian words for surfing are *he'e nalu*, or "wave sliding." In the 1960s, movies and TV shows helped make surfing popular all over the world.

The first Polynesian settlers probably reached Hawai'i in giant **outrigger** canoes. Today, many Hawaiians belong to outrigger clubs. These clubs hold races in the waters around the islands. The missionaries outlawed outrigger canoe racing because the Hawaiians liked to bet on who would win. King Kalākaua revived the sport in 1876. Hawai'i's first outrigger canoe clubs were founded in 1908. The Hawaiian Canoe Racing Association, founded in 1950, sets the rules for racing in the islands.

GEORGE FREETH: RIDING THE WAVES

Early in the 20th century, George Freeth of Honolulu (1883–1919) revived the ancient Polynesian art of surfing. He dazzled onlookers as he rode the waves to shore, standing on an 8-foot (2.4-m) plank. His feats earned him the nickname "The Man Who Walked on Water." Freeth also invented a torpedo-shaped rescue buoy that is now used all over the world.

? **Want to know more?** See www.surfmuseum.org/html/george_freeth1.html

WORD TO KNOW

outrigger *canoes that use floats attached to the hull to help them remain stable in the water*

An outrigger canoe racing off Waikīkī Beach

MICHELLE WIE: THE WIZARD OF THE LINKS

When Michelle Wie (1989–) was four, her father took her to a golf course near their home in Honolulu. She was fascinated by the game and showed signs of unusual talent. By the time she was 11, she was winning every junior event she entered. In 2002, she became the youngest semifinalist in the history of the U.S. Women's Amateur Public Links Championship. Wie began to play professionally in 2004, when she entered her first PGA event. She became the youngest member of the U.S. team in the history of the Curtis Cup Championship, and helped the United States defeat Ireland and the United Kingdom. Wie says she practices golf four hours a day on weekdays and seven hours a day on weekends!

? Want to know more? See http://sports.espn.go.com/golf/players/profile?playerId=1187

Swimming, sailing, snorkeling, scuba diving, and fishing are all popular sports in Hawai'i. Hawai'i also offers plenty of opportunities for hiking, bicycling, and horseback riding.

Hawaiians enjoy team sports such as baseball, basketball, and football. The University of Hawai'i belongs to the Western Athletic Conference of collegiate sports. Each year, an all-star cast of players competes in the Pro Bowl game of the National Football League at Aloha Stadium in Honolulu.

TITLE IX

For a long time, collegiate sports all across the country were played only by men. In 1972, Hawai'i congresswoman Patsy T. Mink helped establish and pass the Patsy T. Mink Equal Opportunity in Education Act, more commonly known as Title IX. This act allowed the establishment of women's collegiate sports teams, athletic, and educational programs throughout the country. Mink's motivation for establishing the act was in part from her own experiences and struggles she faced with gender issues at the University of Hawai'i. Today, Title IX protects the rights of all people to equal education, regardless of their gender.

EDUCATION

King Kamehameha III established the public school system in Hawai'i in 1840. Hawai'i is the only state

Hawaiian high school students

that has a single statewide board of education. Today, all children in Hawai'i must attend school between the ages of six and 17.

The oldest and best-known private academy in Hawai'i is the Punahou School. It was founded in 1841 for the children of missionaries and business owners. Since its opening, though, Native Hawaiian children have been able to attend. Hawai'i has many bilingual schools where classes are taught in Japanese, Chinese, Tagalog, or Korean, as well as in English.

The main campus of the University of Hawai'i is in Honolulu. The university also has campuses in Hilo and West O'ahu. The university has outstanding programs in astronomy, Asian-Pacific studies, and oceanography. Other colleges and universities in Hawai'i include a branch of Utah's Brigham Young University in Laie, O'ahu; and Chaminade University in Honolulu.

At work and at play, the people of Hawai'i celebrate their diversity. They welcome visitors in the spirit of aloha.

THE KAMEHAMEHA SCHOOLS

Bernice Pauahi Bishop was a great-granddaughter of Kamehameha I, and the wife of a wealthy haole banker. When she died in 1884, she left money to found schools for Native Hawaiian children. Her legacy established the Kamehameha Schools in Honolulu. These elementary and high schools offer a quality education to Hawaiian and part-Hawaiian children from throughout the islands.

READ ABOUT

Governor Linda Lingle, with other state officials, addresses the media in October 2006.

CHAPTER SEVEN

GOVERNMENT

★

BEFORE HAWAI'I COULD BECOME A STATE, IT HAD TO DESIGN A CONSTITUTION, OR SET OF GOVERNING LAWS. Hawai'i's constitution seeks to balance the diverse needs of the state's people. It tries to fulfill the philosophy of the state motto: "The life of the land is **perpetuated** in **righteousness**" (*"Ua mau ke ea o ka aina i ka pono"*). That means that a positive attitude, with love, spirit, respect, and honor, should govern the actions of Hawai'i and its citizens at all times.

WORDS TO KNOW

perpetuated *carried on into the future or forward*

righteousness *to be morally just and honest*

In the center of the capitol courtyard is a mosaic called *Aquarius*, made of 6 million tiny colored tiles!

Capitol Facts

Here are some fascinating facts about Hawai'i's state capitol.

- Hawai'i's state capitol is designed to suggest a volcano. The open courtyard in the center represents a volcanic crater.
- The capitol is surrounded by a reflecting pool, representing the Pacific Ocean, which surrounds the state.
- Forty pillars support the roof of the capitol. They resemble coconut palms because the coconut was so important to the early Native Hawaiians.
- The capitol has two main entrances. One faces seaward (makai), and one faces the mountains (mauka).
- The capitol was completed in 1969. Construction cost almost $24.6 million. A renovation to improve the capitol's facilities was done in 1995, costing another $67 million!

THE SEAT OF GOVERNMENT

Hawai'i, the island state, is unique in many ways. It's only fitting that its state capitol is unlike any other. Most state capitols have a high, gilded dome. Hawai'i's building in Honolulu has a broad, open courtyard in the center. The "dome" is the wide Hawaiian sky.

THE EXECUTIVE BRANCH

Before Hawai'i could become a state in 1959, it had to design a constitution, or set of governing laws. The constitution divides the state government into three main branches: executive, legislative, and judicial. The

Hawai'i's capitol

Capital City

This map shows places of interest in Honolulu, Hawai'i's capital city.

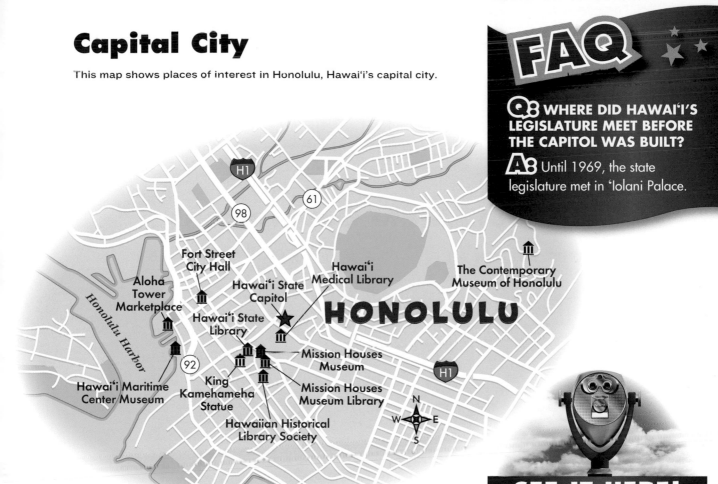

executive branch consists of the office of the governor. The governor is the state's chief executive. The governor and the lieutenant governor are both elected by the people of Hawai'i.

One of the governor's duties is to appoint officials to head important departments in the state government. The governor appoints other members of the executive branch, including the attorney general and finance director. He or she also appoints judges to the highest state courts.

SEE IT HERE!

WASHINGTON PLACE

Until 2002, Washington Place in Honolulu served as the governor's mansion. The building was completed in 1847. Queen Lili'uokalani lived here for many years, until her death in 1917. The foundation and lower walls are made of coral stone. The mansion is square with two verandas and columns on its upper story. There are four parlors on the first floor and four bedrooms on the second. The new Governor's Mansion stands on the grounds of Washington Place.

One of the issues that the governor's office has dealt with for years is the overall prosperity of the state's economy. For many years, unemployment had been a growing problem in Hawai'i. Governor Linda Lingle helped strengthen the economy by creating more employment opportunities and by eliminating the state's overall debt.

Hawai'i State Government

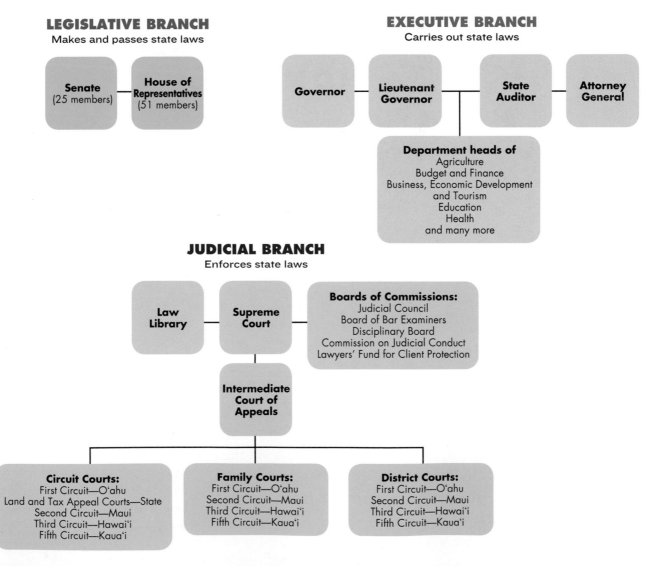

LEGISLATIVE BRANCH
Makes and passes state laws

Senate (25 members)

House of Representatives (51 members)

EXECUTIVE BRANCH
Carries out state laws

Governor

Lieutenant Governor

State Auditor

Attorney General

Department heads of
Agriculture
Budget and Finance
Business, Economic Development and Tourism
Education
Health
and many more

JUDICIAL BRANCH
Enforces state laws

Law Library

Supreme Court

Boards of Commissions:
Judicial Council
Board of Bar Examiners
Disciplinary Board
Commission on Judicial Conduct
Lawyers' Fund for Client Protection

Intermediate Court of Appeals

Circuit Courts:
First Circuit—O'ahu
Land and Tax Appeal Courts—State
Second Circuit—Maui
Third Circuit—Hawai'i
Fifth Circuit—Kaua'i

Family Courts:
First Circuit—O'ahu
Second Circuit—Maui
Third Circuit—Hawai'i
Fifth Circuit—Kaua'i

District Courts:
First Circuit—O'ahu
Second Circuit—Maui
Third Circuit—Hawai'i
Fifth Circuit—Kaua'i

The Hawai'i senate begins a legislative session.

DANIEL K. INOUYE: VETERAN OF THE 442ND

In 1943, Daniel K. Inouye (1924—) was enlisted in the U.S. Army's Nisei 442nd Regimental Combat Team. He served heroically in France and Italy, and lost his right arm in combat. In 2000, he was awarded the Congressional Medal of Honor by President Bill Clinton. Inouye was elected to the U.S. House of Representatives in 1959 and to the Senate in 1962. He has been elected to seven Senate terms. He was the first Japanese American ever to serve in either house of Congress.

? Want to know more? See www.senate. gov/~inouye/bio.html

THE LEGISLATIVE BRANCH

Hawai'i's legislative branch consists of a state legislature with two sections, or houses. The upper house is called the senate. The lower house is called the house of representatives. The legislature meets once a year. Its annual session begins on the third Wednesday in January and lasts for 60 business days.

THE JUDICIAL BRANCH

The judicial branch of Hawai'i's government is the court system. Hawai'i has four district courts, four circuit courts, a family court, land courts, and tax appeal courts. An intermediate court of appeals has five associate judges and a chief judge. The highest court in the state is the supreme court, which is held at 'Iolani Palace. The supreme court has a chief justice and four associate justices.

WEIRD LAWS IN HAWAI'I

- It is illegal to appear in public wearing only swimming trunks.
- It is against the law to own a mongoose without a permit.
- You can be fined if you don't own a boat.
- It is illegal to put pennies in your ears.

Representing Hawai'i

This list shows the number of elected officials who represent Hawai'i, on both the state and national levels.

OFFICE	NUMBER	LENGTH OF TERM
State senators	25	4 years
State representatives	51	2 years
U.S. senators	2	6 years
U.S. representatives	2	2 years
Presidential electors	4	—

LOCAL GOVERNMENT

Hawai'i's towns and cities do not have their own mayors and councils. Instead, each is governed by the county where it is located.

The seven inhabited islands of Hawai'i are divided into four counties. These counties are Hawai'i, Honolulu, Kaua'i, and Maui. These counties are governed by a mayor and an elected council.

Hawai'i's Counties

This map shows the four counties in Hawai'i. Honolulu, the state capital, is indicated with a star.

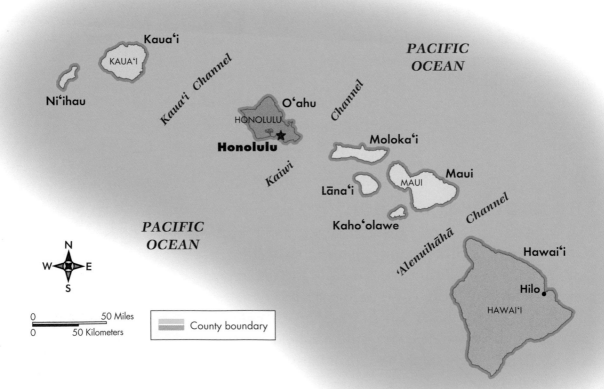

Hawai'i's three branches of government form a system of checks and balances. No single branch is allowed to become too powerful. For instance, the legislative branch may write or enact a new law, which can then be "checked" and either signed or vetoed by the executive branch. The judicial branch can check both branches by determining if a particular power, law, or act is constitutional. Working together, the three branches keep state government running smoothly for the benefit of everyone.

A statue of King Kamehameha I stands outside the supreme court building in Honolulu.

DANIEL KAHIKINA AKAKA: THE TEACHER IN THE SENATE

Daniel Kahikina Akaka (1924–) taught school in Honolulu from 1953 to 1960 and then became a school principal. In 1976, he was elected to the U.S. House of Representatives. He joined the Senate in 1990 and has served three elected terms, during which he has been a member of multiple committees including the Energy and Natural Resources Committee, the Veterans' Affairs Committee, and the Indian Affairs Committee. Akaka is of mixed Chinese and Native Hawaiian ancestry. He is the second Native Hawaiian and the first Chinese American to serve in Congress.

❓ **Want to know more?** See http://akaka.senate. gov/public/index.cfm?FuseAction=Akaka.Home

State Flag

The eight horizontal stripes on Hawai'i's flag represent the eight major islands. The British Union Jack is in the upper left corner. The British flag is included because many of King Kamehameha I's advisers were British, and the islands were once under British protection. The flag has served the kingdom, republic, territory, and state of Hawai'i.

State Seal

The state seal was designed by Viggo Jacobsen when Hawaiʻi was still a republic in 1894. (Jacobsen won a $50 prize with his contest-winning design.) The seal is a modified version of the royal coat of arms. Where the royal seal once had two warriors, the state seal pictures King Kamehameha I on one side. On the other side is the Goddess of Liberty holding the Hawaiian flag. The regal crown was replaced by a rising sun and the year 1959, when Hawaiʻi became a state. The star, which represents Hawaiʻi's star in the American flag, replaced canoe paddles crossed against a sail in the center of the shield.

The state motto is also written on the shield. It reads, *"Ua mau ke ea o ka aina i ka pono,"* which means "The life of the land is perpetuated in righteousness."

READ ABOUT

Enjoying Hawai'i's
beaches is a
favorite pastime of
many vacationers.

CHAPTER EIGHT

ECONOMY

★

A VACATION IN HAWAI'I! What could be more inviting? Your family might save up for years to take such a trip. Or you could get lucky and win a Hawaiian vacation as a prize in a contest or on a game show—but that would be rare. Hawai'i's enchanting beaches, tropical forests, and spectacular mountains have lured visitors for more than a century. No wonder tourism is the leading factor in Hawai'i's economy today.

Restaurants and shops are some of the many tourism-related businesses in Hawai'i.

About 6 million tourists visit Hawai'i each year. That's more than four times the number of people who live in the state!

DOING THINGS FOR OTHERS

People who provide services to others are said to work in the service industries. The check-in clerk at a Maui hotel, a teacher in Hilo, or a shopkeeper in Lahaina are all performing services. Hawai'i's service industries account for about 90 percent of the gross state product (GSP). The GSP is the total value of goods and services produced in a state in a given year. In no other state are the service industries such a large part of the economy!

About one-fifth of Hawai'i's GSP comes from tourism. Tourism-related businesses include hotels, restaurants, stores, boat and car rentals, and guided tours.

The U.S. government is the single largest employer of Hawai'i's service industries. The largest group of government employees works for the military. Every branch of the military has bases on Oʻahu. These include the army's Fort Shafter, Hickam Air Force Base, MCB Hawaiʻi (Marine Corps), and Naval Station Pearl Harbor. All of the U.S. military bases in Hawaiʻi are under the U.S. Pacific Command at Camp H. M. Smith on Oʻahu.

Many Hawaiians who work in the service economy hold jobs in community, business, and personal services. They work in hospitals, law firms, and engineering companies. A growing number of Hawaiians work for companies that develop computer software. Real estate, banking, and the insurance industry are other areas of the service economy where many Hawaiians work.

THE HIGH COST OF LIVING IN PARADISE

With its gentle climate, beautiful scenery, and friendly people, Hawaiʻi is a wonderful place to live. But life in Hawaiʻi comes with a hefty price tag. It costs 30 to 60 percent more to live in Hawaiʻi than it does to live on the U.S. mainland! Housing and food in Hawaiʻi are very expensive. Hawaiʻi imports about 90 percent of its food, which causes the price to stay high.

MINI-BIO

CHARLES REED BISHOP: AN ENDURING LEGACY

Charles Reed Bishop (1822–1915) was a clever businessman. He founded the Bank of Hawaiʻi, the first bank on the islands. Bishop became very wealthy. He and his wife, Bernice Pauahi Bishop, chose to share much of their fortune with future generations of Hawaiians. Bishop helped to establish the Kamehameha Schools in fulfillment of his wife's dream. He also founded Honolulu's Bernice Pauahi Bishop Museum in her memory. The museum features Hawaiian native and cultural history, a science center, and the Hawaiʻi Sports Hall of Fame.

? Want to know more? See www.ksbe.edu/pauahi/crbishop.php

A roadside stand in Maui offers smoothies made with local fruits.

What Do Hawaiians Do?

This color-coded chart shows what industries Hawaiians work in.

18.8% Educational, health and social services, 109,556

15.6% Arts, entertainment, recreation, accommodation, and food services, 91,093

12.1% Retail trade, 70,369

9.4% Professional, scientific, management, administrative, and waste management services, 54,983

8.3% Public administration, 48,346

7.9% Construction, 46,085

7.5% Finance, insurance, real estate and rental and leasing, 43,416

5.6% Transportation and warehousing, and utilities, 32,823

5.0% Other services (except public administration), 28,985

3.4% Manufacturing, 19,685

3.1% Wholesale trade, 18,163

2.0% Information, 11,632

1.3% Agriculture, forestry, fishing and hunting, and mining, 7,595

Source: U.S. Census Bureau, 2005 estimate

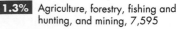

AGRICULTURE

Sugarcane and pineapples were once the mainstays of Hawai'i's economy. They are still among the most valuable crops grown in Hawai'i today. Maui leads the other islands in both sugar and pineapple production. These two crops combined account for more than 25 percent of Hawai'i's income from agriculture.

Approximately one-third of Hawai'i's land is used for farming. The state has about 5,500 farms. However, large corporations control most of the farmland on the

Pineapples being harvested by machine in Maui

THE MAN BEHIND THE MACHINE

When a truckload of prickly, fresh pineapples arrives at the processing plant, the fruit must be peeled and cored. Each pineapple is sent through a machine called a ginaca. The ginaca strips off the spiny hull, carves out the core, and slices off the fruit's tough ends. This marvelous machine was named for its inventor, Henry Gabriel Ginaca (1876–1918). Ginaca was born in California. As a young man, he moved to Honolulu, where he worked as a mechanical engineer. In 1911, James Dole hired him to invent a machine for processing pineapple. Ginaca's machine was very successful. It could prepare 50 pineapples in an hour. Only 15 could be peeled and cored by hand in the same amount of time.

Top Products

Manufacturing Processed food, refined petroleum, printed materials, glass and stone products, jewelry, clothing

Agriculture Greenhouse and nursery products, sugarcane, pineapples, coffee, bananas, avocados, papayas, guavas, taro, cattle, hogs, poultry, eggs

Fishing Yellowfin and bigeye tuna, aquaculture products (shellfish and algae)

Hawai'i's Major Agricultural and Mining Products

This map shows where Hawai'i's major agricultural and mining products come from. See a pineapple? That means pineapples are found there.

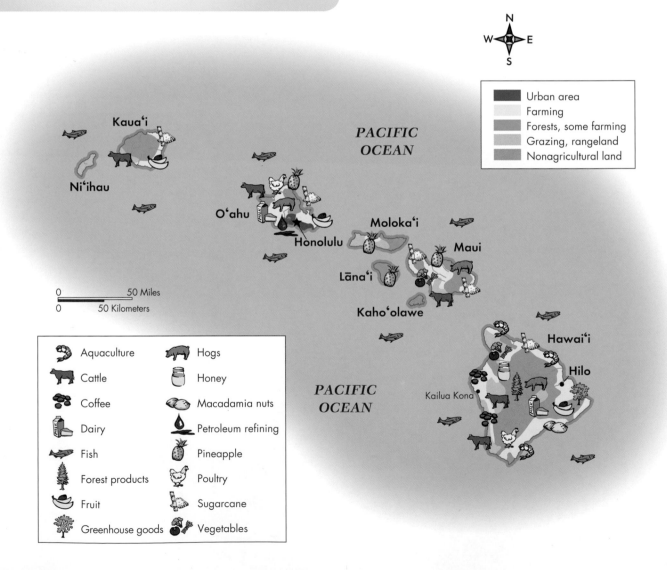

Urban area
Farming
Forests, some farming
Grazing, rangeland
Nonagricultural land

Aquaculture
Cattle
Coffee
Dairy
Fish
Forest products
Fruit
Greenhouse goods

Hogs
Honey
Macadamia nuts
Petroleum refining
Pineapple
Poultry
Sugarcane
Vegetables

A rancher herds cattle on the Big Island.

islands. The entire island of Ni'ihau is privately owned and for years was used for cattle raising.

Farms operate on all of Hawai'i's inhabited islands Coffee is a major crop grown for export. Other exported farm products include tropical fruits such as avocados, guavas, papayas, and bananas. Some small farms raise vegetables for local markets. Orchids are raised for sale to florists on the U.S. mainland.

Hawaiian farmers also raise cattle, pigs, and poultry. Several large cattle ranches operate on the island of Hawai'i.

NUTS TO HAWAI'I!

In 1882, William H. Purvis, a sugar planter from Hawai'i, visited Australia. He noticed a lovely tree that bore delicious nuts. Purvis brought some macadamia nuts, as they were called, back to Hawai'i. He planted them at Kapulena on the Big Island and raised the trees because he liked the way they looked. During the 1950s, commercial growers realized there could be a market for the nuts. Today, you can munch dry-roasted macadamia nuts or enjoy them in candy or cookies. Some 90 percent of the world's macadamia nuts are grown in Hawai'i.

KING'S HAWAIIAN BREAD

Robert Taira (1923–2003) was a young man, born to Hawaiian immigrant parents from Japan. After serving in the U.S. Armed Services, Taira attended baking schools in Hilo, Hawai'i, and Chicago, Illinois. By the 1950s, he was ready to start his own bakery, and with only $382 (which he borrowed from his family), he founded the King's Hawaiian Bread Co. Today, King's Hawaiian Bread is one of the world's finest purveyors of baked goods and one of Hawaii's most successful local businesses.

Workers handle peeled and cored pineapple along an assembly line at a Dole cannery.

MANUFACTURING INDUSTRY

Hawai'i's pineapple industry gave rise to another major business on the islands: fruit canning. Hawai'i processes pineapples, cans them, and ships them all over the world. The islands also have many sugar refineries. There, raw sugarcane is turned into the sugar you might sprinkle on your breakfast cereal. Other processed foods from Hawai'i include bread, candy, cheese, and fruit juice.

FISHING

Fishing has been part of life in Hawai'i since the first Polynesian voyagers arrived. Today, fishing is both sport and big business. The most important commercial catches are bigeye and yellowfin tuna.

Hawai'i has also begun to develop **aquaculture** in its offshore waters. Ocean farmers raise shellfish and some kinds of edible seaweed, which is chiefly sold to markets in Japan.

WORD TO KNOW

aquaculture *farming of fish, shellfish, and plants that live in water*

Workers handle fresh fish at a market in Hilo.

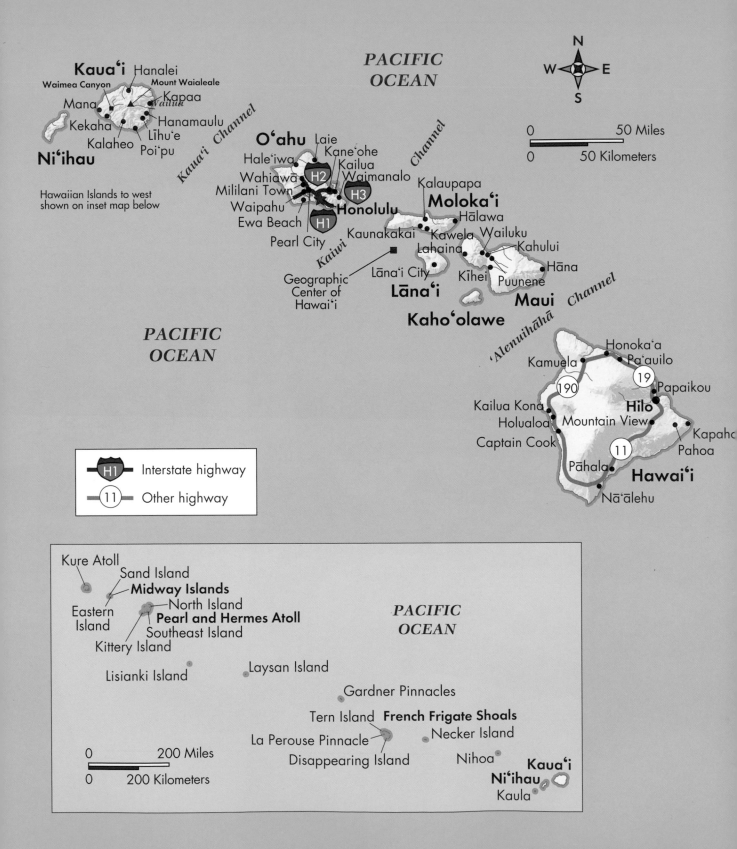

PACIFIC OCEAN

N
W E
S

Kaua'i
Hanalei
Waimea Canyon   Mount Waialeale
Mana   Kapaa
Wailua
Kekaha   Hanamaulu
Kalaheo   Līhu'e
Ni'ihau   Poi'pu

Hawaiian Islands to west
shown on inset map below

0   50 Miles
0   50 Kilometers

O'ahu   Laie
Kane'ohe
Hale'iwa   Kailua
Wahiawā   Waimanalo
Mililani Town   **H3**
Waipahu   **H2**
Ewa Beach   **H1**   **Honolulu**   **Moloka'i**   Kalaupapa
Pearl City   Hālawa
Kaunakakai   Kawela   Wailuku
Geographic   Lahaina   Kahului
Center of   **Lāna'i City**   Kīhei   Hāna
Hawai'i   **Lāna'i**   Puunene
Kaho'olawe   **Maui**

Channel
Kaua'i Channel
Kaiwi
'Alenuihāhā Channel

PACIFIC OCEAN

Honoka'a
Kamuela   Pa'auilo
190   19   Papaikou
Kailua Kona   **Hilo**
Holualoa   Mountain View
Captain Cook   Kapaho
11   Pahoa
Pāhala   **Hawai'i**
Nā'ālehu

Interstate highway
H1   Interstate highway
11   Other highway

Kure Atoll
Sand Island
Midway Islands
North Island
Eastern   **Pearl and Hermes Atoll**
Island   Southeast Island
Kittery Island

Lisianki Island   Laysan Island

Gardner Pinnacles

Tern Island   **French Frigate Shoals**
La Perouse Pinnacle   Necker Island
Disappearing Island   Nihoa   **Kaua'i**
Ni'ihau
Kaula

PACIFIC OCEAN

0   200 Miles
0   200 Kilometers

CHAPTER NINE

TRAVEL GUIDE

TRAVEL GUIDE

★

Hawai'i offers a rare blend of natural wonders, historic sites, and cultural treasures. When you visit the Aloha State, you will travel from beaches to mountains, from barren deserts to the teeming capital city. You will move from island to island by boat or small plane, always aware of the vast ocean around you. Here are some of the highlights you may experience on the main Hawaiian islands.

← Follow along with this travel map. We'll begin on Kaua'i and travel all around and finish on Hawai'i, the Big Island.

KAUAʻI, THE GARDEN ISLAND

THINGS TO DO: Visit lush forests, tour beautiful gardens, and learn about ancient temples.

★ **Alakaʻi Swamp:** This region is a wet, steamy jungle with muddy streams and boot-sucking bogs. Don't forget to wear long sleeves and bring plenty of mosquito repellent!

★ **Waimea Canyon:** This canyon is a deep gorge west of Mount Waiʻaleʻale. Its dramatic rock formations remind some visitors of Arizona's famous Grand Canyon.

★ **Limahuli Gardens:** Located north of the town of Hanaleʻi, these gardens have everything from glorious wildflowers to taro fields.

A climber above Alakaʻi Swamp

★ **National Tropical Botanical Gardens:** These gardens at Poiʻpu contain a special collection of herbs once used by the Native Hawaiians for healing the sick.

★ **Hikinaʻaka Temple:** At this temple near the mouth of the Wailua River, kahunas once chanted special prayers to the rising sun. Not far from the temple is an enclosure that served as a refuge for those in danger. Its gates were always open to welcome defeated warriors and people who had broken the kapu. Once inside the refuge, they were safe.

Limahuli Gardens

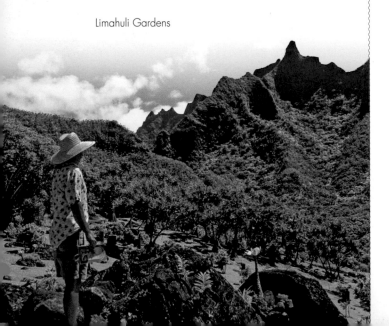

NI'IHAU, THE FORBIDDEN ISLE

In 1864, an American woman named Elizabeth Sinclair Robinson bought Ni'ihau from the Kingdom of Hawai'i. To this day, the island belongs to the Robinson family. It has been closed to most outsiders since 1915. For this reason, it is often called the Forbidden Isle.

Until 1999, the Robinson family used Ni'ihau as a cattle and sheep ranch. The family has begun to open the island to limited tourism. Hunters, fishers, and sightseers may make day trips to Ni'ihau and explore this mysterious island.

★ **Altar to Kāne:** At the top of Mount Wai'ale'ale stands a stone altar to the Hawaiian god Kāne. Kāne was the god of light and living things. Once a year, priests and chiefs made their way up the mountainside, climbing through the tangled forest. At the altar, they made sacrifices to Kāne while musicians played flutes and beat drums.

SEE IT HERE!

NI'IHAU LEIS

Ni'ihau is too dry to grow tropical flowers. For centuries, the people here have made leis from tiny shells. Today, many Native Hawaiians on Ni'ihau gather shells and make leis and delicate shell jewelry for sale.

Ni'ihau

JONAH KŪHIŌ KALANIANA'OLE: THE PRINCE WHO WENT TO WASHINGTON

Prince Jonah Kūhiō Kalaniana'ole (1871–1922) grew up on Kaua'i and O'ahu. As the adopted son of King Kalākaua's wife, Kalaniana'ole was a royal prince. He left Hawai'i to study in California and Great Britain, but later returned to his homeland. After Hawai'i became a U.S. territory, he went to Congress as a nonvoting representative. He served in Congress from 1903 until his death in 1922.

? Want to know more? See www.aloha-hawaii. com/hawaii/prine+kuhio/

Kuhio Beach Park

O'AHU, THE GATHERING PLACE

THINGS TO DO: See the sights in the capital city, explore the island's mountains and beaches and the state's biggest city.

Honolulu

★ **Waikīkī Beach:** Flanked by luxury hotels, Waikīkī Beach appears in movies, magazines, and advertisements for Hawaiian vacations. When you've had enough swimming and sunbathing, visit Waikiki's outstanding aquarium. It displays small sharks and many other kinds of fish found in local waters.

★ **Kūhiō Beach Park:** This park is named after Prince Jonah Kūhiō Kalaniana'ole. Once the site of Kūhiō's home, it is now a public beach and features a statue of Kūhiō.

★ **Hawai'i Children's Discovery Center:** The whole family can explore hands-on exhibits about marine life, astronomy, archaeology, and much more.

★ **Hawai'i State Art Museum:** To the people of Honolulu, this museum is known as HISAM. Its exhibits portray the state's history and culture through painting, sculpture, and photography.

★ **Mission Houses Museum:** Walk through three fully restored homes where some of the early Protestant missionaries once lived. The museum includes a working replica of the 1820 printing press used to print the Bible in the Hawaiian language.

★ **Bernice Pauahi Bishop Museum:** This remarkable museum tells the story of Hawai'i through several halls of permanent and special exhibits. Polynesian Hall is a two-story gallery with displays about the many cultures of the Pacific Islands. The Kahili Room honors the chiefs of Hawai'i. It preserves their weapons, portraits, and beautiful feather banners. The museum's Science Adventure Center has many absorbing interactive displays. The Science Center emphasizes Hawai'i's contributions to the study of volcanoes and marine life. The Hawai'i Sports Hall of Fame commemorates the achievements of the state's leading athletes.

★ **Hawai'i Heritage Center:** Learn about the history of Honolulu's Chinatown and the immigrants who have lived there over the years.

Bernice Pauahi Bishop Museum

★ **Japanese Cultural Center of Hawai'i:** Photos and other memorabilia of Japanese immigrant life are on display.

★ **Law Enforcement Museum:** Displays trace the history of the Honolulu Police Department. The museum contains photos and memorabilia related to Detective Chang Apana, the model for the fictional detective Charlie Chan.

SEE IT HERE!

THE FALLS OF CLYDE

The Falls of Clyde is the world's last iron-hulled fully rigged four-masted sailing ship! It was built in Scotland in 1878 and is still afloat at the Hawai'i Maritime Center in Honolulu.

Sea Life Park

Laie

★ **Polynesian Cultural Center:** Seven ancient villages have been reconstructed at this museum. Women and men in traditional costumes demonstrate kapa weaving, canoe making, taro grinding, and other activities.

A traditional ceremony at the Polynesian Cultural Center

Waimanalo

★ **Sea Life Park:** This is a great place to learn about the animals that live in the ocean around Hawai'i. A saltwater aquarium houses a dazzling variety of colorful fish. A bird sanctuary within the park is home to many kinds of shorebirds. Performances by dolphins and small whales are a favorite attraction.

Hale'iwa

★ **North Shore Surf and Cultural Museum:** If you have a taste for old surfer movies, you can watch them all day long at this unusual museum! It also has a collection of antique surfboards.

MOLOKA'I, THE FRIENDLY ISLE

THINGS TO DO: Hit the beach, see African wildlife, and visit a historic park.

★ **Moloka'i Ranch:** Learn about Hawai'i's ranching and plantation past by visiting this working ranch and former pineapple plantation. On these 53,000 acres (21,500 ha), you can go horseback riding and kayaking or find time to hit the golf course.

★ **Kalaupapa National Historical Park:** This park lies on a slender peninsula beneath steep, looming cliffs. The park is the site of a former colony for people with leprosy, or Hansen's disease. A visit to the park usually begins with a heart-stopping mule ride down the cliffs. Former residents of the colony lead guided tours. You can see St. Joseph's Church, where the sick once worshipped, and walk through the simple houses where they lived. Today, Hansen's disease can be treated successfully. People with this disease are no longer forced to live apart.

FATHER DAMIEN, JOSEPH DE VEUSTER: THE MARTYR OF MOLOKA'I

Leprosy, or Hansen's disease, first appeared in Hawai'i around 1830. People with the disease often developed severe body deformities. Healthy people dreaded catching the disease. To prevent its spread, infected persons were sent to live in an isolated colony on Moloka'i. In 1873, a priest from Belgium, Father Damien (1840–1889), went to Moloka'i and offered his help. He encouraged the people of the colony to start small businesses, to build a church, and to live as fully as possible. Father Damien caught Hansen's disease himself and died of it at the age of 49. After his death, he was remembered as "the Martyr of Moloka'i."

? Want to know more? See www.newadvent. org/cathen/04615a.htm

Kalaupapa National Historical Park

LANA'I, THE PINEAPPLE ISLAND

THINGS TO DO: Explore the ruins of a former fishing village and watch cliff divers leap into the ocean.

★ **Kaunolu:** Here you can visit the remains of a once-thriving fishing village. Eighty-six platforms cut into the cliffside mark the places where the villagers built their homes. Signs along a trail through the village point out places of interest. Take a look at the high, jutting rock from which daring young divers used to leap 62 feet (19 m) into the sea! Making the leap was seen as proof of courage and strength.

SEE IT HERE!

HAUOLA STONE

On the shore, in front of Lahaina's Public Library, is a large stone shaped like a seat with a low back. It is called the Hauola Stone. Native Hawaiian kahunas used to send sick people to sit on the stone and dangle their feet in the water. The stone was thought to have healing powers.

MAUI, THE VALLEY ISLE

THINGS TO DO: Hike up a volcano, check out an ancient ship, and visit a black sand beach.

★ **Haleakalā:** Soaring 10,023 feet (3,055 m), this is Maui's highest peak. If you drive to the top early in the morning, you can watch the sunrise above the mountain's vast volcanic crater.

★ ***Carthaginian II* Floating Museum:** Have you ever wondered what life was like aboard a 19th-century ship? Hawai'i's early missionaries arrived in ships much like the *Carthaginian II*. The museum is a fully restored sailing vessel anchored at Lahaina. It offers exhibits on whaling and the lives and habits of whales.

Carthaginian II Floating Museum

An exhibit at the Hana Cultural Center and Museum

★ **Hana Cultural Center and Museum:** This museum on Hana Bay is a treasure chest of Hawaiian history. Its collection includes Hawaiian quilts, dyed kapa fabric, stone and bone tools, and hollowed-out boards used for pounding taro into poi.

★ **Waiʻanapanapa State Park:** This park is a popular seaside resort. The black sand of the beach is made of crushed lava stone. Throughout the park, volcanic stone forms a maze of arches, tunnels, and caverns. By diving through an underwater tunnel, you can enter a large, hidden cave. According to legend, two young women were once murdered here. One was a princess named Popoʻalaea, and the other was her devoted maid, Manona. Popoʻalaea's husband killed them both in a jealous rage. Every spring, schools of shrimp turn the stones of the cave bloodred, as though to remember the ancient tragedy.

★ **Loaloa Temple:** Surrounded by high walls, this ancient temple at Kaupo looks like a fortress. According to legend, it was built by the menehune, a mysterious race of tiny people who lived in the forests. Local people claim that small footprints can be seen in lava rock 13 miles (20 km) from the temple. They say these prints were left by the menehune as they hauled massive stones to the building site.

FAQ

Q: WHO WERE THE MENEHUNE?

A: Nobody knows for sure. Some scientists think that Hawaiʻi's first settlers were people of fairly short stature. Later arrivals may have been much taller, giving rise to the menehune legend.

Waiʻanapanapa State Park

KAHO'OLAWE, THE SMALLEST ISLAND

The tiny island of Kaho'olawe is separated from Maui by a narrow channel. Kaho'olawe was a place of deep religious meaning to the ancient Hawaiians. Since the arrival of Europeans and Americans, the island has had a troubled history.

From 1826 to 1853, Kaho'olawe served as a prison colony. Later, ranchers brought in flocks of sheep and goats. The animals stripped the island of native grasses and other plants. From 1941 until 1993, the U.S. military used the island for target practice. The island was battered with bombs and artillery shells.

In 1994, Congress returned Kaho'olawe to the state of Hawai'i. The transfer was completed in 2003.

The Kaho'olawe Island Reserve Commission is working to restore the island's native plant life. The commission is also trying to rescue archaeological sites that were damaged by the military. Kaho'olawe is not yet open to visitors. Hawaiians hope that it will someday be green and healthy again.

FAQ ★ ★ ★

Q8 HOW MANY PEOPLE LIVE ON KAHO'OLAWE?

A8 Kaho'olawe is uninhabited today.

Kaho'olawe contains 544 archaeological and historic sites!

HAWAI'I, THE BIG ISLAND

THINGS TO DO: Investigate volcanoes, see Hawaiian cowboys, and visit historic museums.

Hilo

★ **Lyman House Memorial Museum:** This museum is the restored home of an early missionary family. The museum includes a fascinating collection of Hawaiian minerals and rocks from around the world.

Lyman House Memorial Museum

★ **Plantation Museum:** A variety of exhibits re-create life on Hawai'i's sugar and coffee plantations.

★ **Laupāhoehoe Train Museum:** If you're a railroad buff, you won't want to miss this one! The museum is a tribute to the Hilo Narrow-gauge Railroad. Narrow-gauge railroads were designed to carry trains through mountainous country over many twists and curves. Here a 1900 narrow-gauge diesel engine runs on a circle of track.

★ **Nani Mau Gardens:** These gardens feature some 2,000 types of orchids from all over the globe.

★ **Akaka Falls State Park:** An easy drive from Hilo, this park preserves a dense rain forest with many native trees and ferns. Highlights are two spectacular waterfalls.

Kamuela

★ **Parker Ranch Museum:** When you think of Hawai'i, you probably don't think of cowboys! Amazingly, Hawai'i has a long cowboy tradition. Experienced Mexican cowherds came to work in Hawai'i's cattle industry in the 1800s. Learn about Hawai'i's cowboys, called *paniolos*, at this museum. On display are historic photos and antique ranching equipment such as saddles, lassos, and branding irons.

Pahoa

★ **Lava Tree State Park:** Imagine a grove of trees frozen in time. At this park, you can see trees that have been encased in lava since a volcanic eruption in 1790!

Lava Tree State Park

WRITING PROJECTS

Check out these ideas for creating a campaign brochure and writing you-are-there narratives. Or research the migration paths of settlers and explorers.

118

ART PROJECTS

You can illustrate the state song, create a dazzling PowerPoint presentation, or learn about the state quarter and design your own.

119

HAWAII
1959

UA MAU
KE EA O KA
ʻĀINA I KA PONO

2008
E PLURIBUS UNUM

TIMELINE

What happened when? This timeline highlights important events in the state's history—and shows what was happening throughout the United States at the same time.

122

FAST FACTS

Use this section to find fascinating facts about state symbols, land area and population statistics, weather, sports teams, and much more.

126

GLOSSARY

Remember the Words to Know from the chapters in this book? They're all collected here.

125

SCIENCE, TECHNOLOGY, & MATH PROJECTS

Make weather maps, learn about population statistics, and research endangered species that live in the state.

120

PRIMARY VS. SECONDARY SOURCES

121

So what are primary and secondary sources? And what's the diff? This section explains all that and where you can find them.

BIOGRAPHICAL DICTIONARY

133

This at-a-glance guide highlights some of the state's most important and influential people. Visit this section and read about their contributions to the state, the country, and the world.

RESOURCES

Books, Web sites, DVDs, and more. Take a look at these additional sources for information about the state.

137

WRITING PROJECTS

★ ★ ★

Write a Memoir, Journal, or Editorial for Your School Newspaper!

Picture Yourself . . .

★ Living as a commoner under the kapu system.

   SEE: Chapter Two, page 26.

★ Spotting Captain Cook's ships arriving in Hawai'i.

   SEE: Chapter Three, pages 33–34.

★ As King Kalākaua on his first trip around the world.

   SEE: Chapter Four, pages 50 and 51.

★ On August 12, 1889, at 'Iolani Palace, as Hawai'i becomes a possession of the United States, and the Hawiian flag is lowered and replaced with the U.S. flag.

   SEE: Chapter Four, page 52.

Create an Election Brochure or Web Site!

Run for office!

Throughout this book, you've read about some of the issues that concern Hawai'i today.

★ As a candidate for governor of Hawai'i, create a campaign brochure or Web site.

★ Explain how you meet the qualifications to be governor of Hawai'i, and talk about the three or four major issues you'll focus on if you're elected.

★ Remember, you'll be responsible for Hawai'i's budget. How would you spend the taxpayers' money.

   SEE: Chapter Seven, pages 84–91.

   GO TO: Hawai'i's government Web site at www.ehawaii.gov/dakine/index.html.

Compare and Contrast—When, Why, and How Did They Come?

Compare the migration and explorations of the first Native people and the first European explorers. Tell about:

★ When their migrations began

★ How they traveled

★ Why they migrated

★ Where their journeys began and ended

★ What they found when they arrived

   SEE: Chapters Two and Three, pages 20–41.

Herb Kawainui Kane's painting
The Discovery of Hawai'i

ART PROJECTS

★ ★ ★

Create a PowerPoint Presentation or Visitors' Guide

Welcome to Hawai'i!

Hawai'i is a great place to visit and to live! From its natural beauty to its historic sites, there's plenty to see and do. In your PowerPoint presentation or brochure, highlight 10 to 15 of Hawai'i's amazing landmarks. Be sure to include:

★ a map of the islands showing where these sites are located

★ photos, illustrations, Web links, natural history facts, geographic stats, climate and weather info, and descriptions of plants and wildlife

SEE: Chapter Nine, pages 104–115.

GO TO: The official Web site of Hawai'i tourism at www.gohawaii.com. Download and print maps, photos, national landmark images, and vacation ideas for tourists.

Illustrate the Lyrics to the Hawai'i State Song

"Hawai'i Ponoi"
("Hawai'i's Own People")

Use markers, paints, photos, collage, colored pencils, or computer graphics to illustrate the lyrics to "Hawai'i Ponoi," the state song. Turn your illustrations into a picture book, or scan them into a PowerPoint and add music!

SEE: The lyrics to "Hawai'i Ponoi" on page 128.

GO TO: The Hawai'i state Web site at www.ehawaii.gov/dakine/index.html to find out more about the origin of "Hawai'i Ponoi."

Research the State Quarter

From 1999 to 2008, the U.S. Mint introduced new quarters commemorating each of the 50 states in the order that they were admitted into the Union. Each state's quarter features a unique design on its reverse, or back.

GO TO: www.usmint.gov/kids and find out what's featured on the back of the Hawai'i quarter.

Research and write an essay explaining:

★ the significance of each image

★ who designed the quarter

★ who chose the final design

Design your own Hawai'i state quarter. What images would you choose for the reverse?

★ Make a poster showing the Hawai'i quarter and label each image.

SCIENCE, TECHNOLOGY, & MATH PROJECTS

★ ★ ★

Graph Population Statistics!

★ Compare population statistics (such as ethnic background, birth, death, and literacy rates) in Hawai'i counties.

★ In your graph or chart, look at population density, and write sentences describing what the population statistics show; graph one set of population statistics, and write a paragraph explaining what the graphs reveal.

SEE: Chapter Six, pages 68–83.

GO TO: The official Web site for the U.S. Census Bureau at www.census.gov, and at http://quickfacts.census.gov/qfd/states/15000.html, to find out more about population statistics, how they work, and what the statistics are for Hawai'i.

Create a Weather Map of Hawai'i!

Use your knowledge of Hawai'i's geography to research and identify conditions that result in specific weather events. Create a weather map or poster that shows the weather patterns over the state. To accompany your map, explain the technology used to measure weather phenomena.

SEE: Chapter One, page 16.

GO TO: The National Oceanic and Atmospheric Administration's National Weather Service Web site at www.weather.gov for weather maps and forecasts for Hawai'i.

Track Endangered Species

Using your knowledge of Hawai'i's wildlife, research what animals and plants are endangered or threatened. Find out what the state is doing to protect these species. Chart known populations of the animals and plants, and report on changes in certain geographic areas.

SEE: Chapter One, page 17.

GO TO: The U.S. Fish and Wildlife site at www.fws.gov/endangered/ or other Hawai'i-specific sites such as www.endangeredspecie.com/states/hi.htm

Students in the city of Lāna'i

PRIMARY VS. SECONDARY SOURCES

★　★　★

What's the Diff?

Your teacher may require at least one or two primary sources and one or two secondary sources for your assignment. So, what's the difference between the two?

★ **Primary sources are original.** You are reading the actual words of someone's diary, journal, letter, autobiography, or interview. Primary sources can also be photographs, maps, prints, cartoons, news/film footage, posters, first-person newspaper articles, drawings, musical scores, and recordings. By the way, when you conduct a survey, interview someone, shoot a video, or take photographs to include in a project—you are creating primary sources!

★ **Secondary sources are what you find in encyclopedias, textbooks, articles, biographies, and almanacs.** These are written by a person or group of people who tell about something that happened to someone else. Secondary sources also recount what another person said or did. This book is an example of a secondary source.

Now that you know what primary sources are—where can you find them?

★ **Your school or local library:** Check the library catalog for collections of original writings, government documents, musical scores, and so on. Some of this material may be stored on microfilm. The Library of Congress Web site (www.loc.gov) is an excellent online resource for primary source materials.

★ **Historical societies:** These organizations keep historical documents, photographs, and other materials. Staff members can help you find what you are looking for. History museums are also great places to see primary sources firsthand.

★ **The Internet:** There are lots of sites that have primary sources you can download and use in a project or assignment.

TIMELINE

★ ★ ★

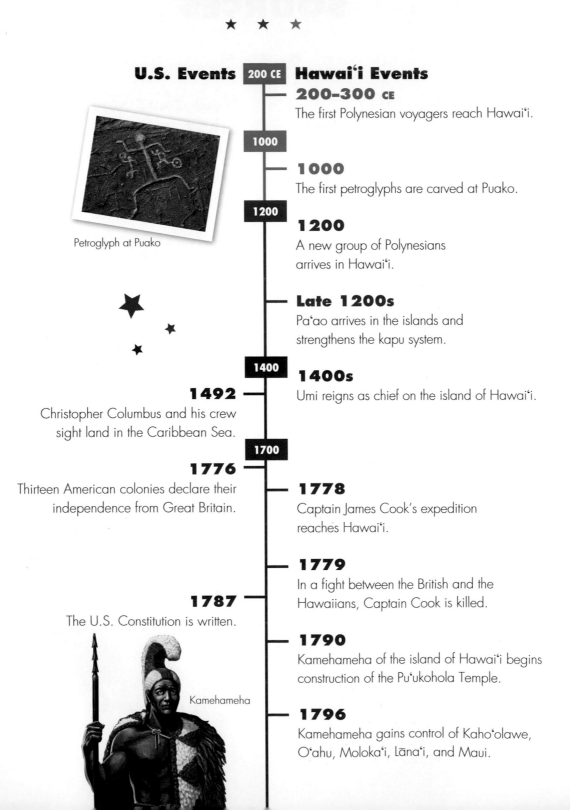

U.S. Events | 200 CE | **Hawai'i Events**

200–300 CE
The first Polynesian voyagers reach Hawai'i.

1000

1000
The first petroglyphs are carved at Puako.

Petroglyph at Puako

1200

1200
A new group of Polynesians arrives in Hawai'i.

Late 1200s
Pa'ao arrives in the islands and strengthens the kapu system.

1400

1400s
Umi reigns as chief on the island of Hawai'i.

1492
Christopher Columbus and his crew sight land in the Caribbean Sea.

1700

1776
Thirteen American colonies declare their independence from Great Britain.

1778
Captain James Cook's expedition reaches Hawai'i.

1779
In a fight between the British and the Hawaiians, Captain Cook is killed.

1787
The U.S. Constitution is written.

1790
Kamehameha of the island of Hawai'i begins construction of the Pu'ukohola Temple.

Kamehameha

1796
Kamehameha gains control of Kaho'olawe, O'ahu, Moloka'i, Lāna'i, and Maui.

U.S. Events	**1800**	Hawai'i Events

1803
The Louisiana Purchase almost doubles the size of the United States.

1810
Kamehameha unites all of the islands as the Kingdom of Hawai'i.

1812–15
The United States and Great Britain fight the War of 1812.

1819
Queen Ka'ahumanu helps brings an end to the kapu system.

1820
The first Protestant missionaries arrive in Hawai'i.

1830
The Indian Removal Act forces eastern Native American groups to relocate west of the Mississippi River.

1830s
Whaling ships begin stopping at Hawaiian ports to take on supplies.

1860s
Sugar plantations become big business on the islands.

1861–65
The American Civil War is fought between the Northern Union and the Southern Confederacy; it ends with the surrender of the Confederate army, led by General Robert E. Lee.

1874
King David Kalākaua is the first ruling monarch to visit the United States.

1886
Apache leader Geronimo surrenders to the U.S. Army, ending the last major Native American rebellion against the expansion of the United States into the West.

1887
Sugar planters pressure the Hawaiian government to accept a new constitution giving more power to foreign landowners and making Pearl Harbor a U.S. naval base.

Lowering the Hawaiian flag outside 'Iolani Palace

1893
A group of planters overthrows Queen Lili'uokalani in a bloodless takeover; the Republic of Hawai'i is established.

1898
The United States gains control of Cuba, Puerto Rico, the Philippines, and Guam after defeating Spain in the Spanish-American War.

1898
Hawai'i becomes a possession of the United States.

U.S. Events	**1900**	Hawai'i Events

1900
Hawai'i becomes a U.S. territory.

1912
The USS *California* is the first large naval vessel to dock at Pearl Harbor.

1917–18
The United States engages in World War I.

1929
The stock market crashes, plunging the United States further into the Great Depression.

1941–45
The United States engages in World War II.

1941
Pearl Harbor is attacked by Japanese bombers, bringing the United States into World War II; Hawai'i is placed under martial law.

1942
The U.S. Army forms the 100th Battalion with Japanese American soldiers.

1951–53
The United States engages in the Korean War.

1959
Hawai'i becomes the 50th state.

1964–73
The United States engages in the Vietnam War.

1991
The United States and other nations engage in the brief Persian Gulf War against Iraq.

1993
President Bill Clinton signs the Apology Resolution, apologizing for the U.S. overthrow of the Kingdom of Hawai'i.

2000

2001
Terrorists hijack four U.S. aircraft and crash them into the World Trade Center in New York City, the Pentagon in Arlington, Virginia, and a Pennsylvania field, killing thousands.

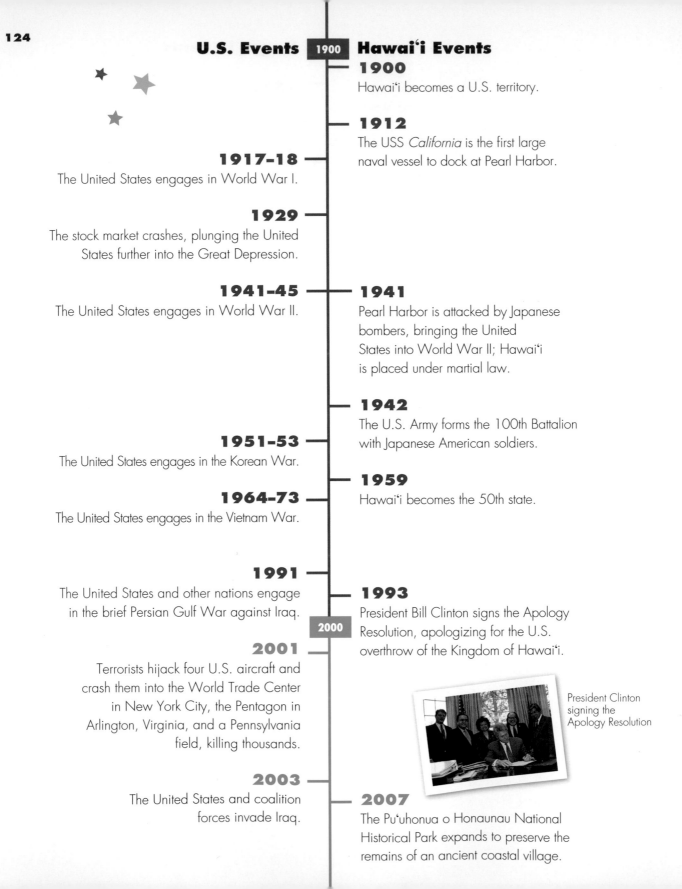

President Clinton signing the Apology Resolution

2003
The United States and coalition forces invade Iraq.

2007
The Pu'uhonua o Honaunau National Historical Park expands to preserve the remains of an ancient coastal village.

GLOSSARY

★ ★ ★

alien foreign

ali'i Hawaiian word for "chiefs"

aloha Hawaiian word of greeting, also meaning a spirit of affection and regard

aquaculture farming of fish, shellfish, and plants that live in water

archipelago chain of islands

breadfruit a large, starchy fruit that grows on trees

converted changed

feral once domesticated but now gone back to the wild

haoles foreign-born Hawaiian islanders (usually Caucasian)

immunity natural protection against disease

kahunas Hawaiian word for "priests"

kapa fabric made from the inner bark of trees

kupu a system of taboos forbidding certain actions

lava melted, or molten, rock that comes from a volcano

magma melted rock that has not yet erupted

maka'aina Hawaiian word for "commoners"

mālama Hawaiian word meaning "to care for"

malos garments worn by Hawaiian men over their lower body

mana Hawaiian word for "power given by the gods"

martial law military law, military control

molten hot enough to melt

monarch king or queen

mural painting on a wall

outrigger canoes that use floats attached to the hull to help them remain stable in the water

perpetuated carried on into the future or forward

petroglyphs pictures carved or painted on stone

Pidgin a language consisting of words and grammar from two or more languages

refining removing impurities; perfecting

righteousness to be morally just and honest

sandalwood heavy, sweet-smelling wood of a tree found in Hawai'i's mountains

sovereign independent, under its own government

taro a vegetable similar to the beet, with leaves and roots that are edible when cooked

tsunamis huge waves caused by undersea or near-shore earthquakes, eruptions, or landslides

FAST FACTS

★ ★ ★

State Symbols

Statehood date	August 21, 1959, the 50th state
Origin of state name	Possibly derived from *hawaiki* or *owyhyhee*, Native words for "homeland"
State capital	Honolulu
State nickname	Aloha State
State motto	*"Ua Mau Ke Ea O Ka Aina I Ka Pono"* ("The Life of the Land Is Perpetuated in Righteousness")
State bird	Nēnē (Hawaiian goose)
State marine mammal	Humpback whale
State flower	Yellow hibiscus
State song	"Hawai'i Ponoi" (See lyrics on page 128)
State tree	Kukui (candlenut)
State gem	Black coral
State fair	Honolulu (May–June)

State seal

Geography

Total area; rank	10,931 square miles (28,311 sq km); 43rd
Land; rank	6,423 square miles (16,635 sq km); 47th
Water; rank	4,508 square miles (11,675 sq km); 13th
Inland water; rank	38 square miles (98 sq km); 50th
Coastal water; rank	590 square miles (1,528 sq km); 10th
Territorial water; rank	4,470 square miles (11,577 km); 4th
Geographic center	Located off the southwestern shore of Moloka'i west of Lāna'i
Latitude	16° 55' N to 23° N
Longitude	154° 40' W to 162° W
Highest point	Pu'u Wēkiu, Mauna Kea, 13,796 feet (4,205 m)
Lowest point	Sea level at the Pacific Ocean
Largest city	Honolulu
Number of counties	4
Longest rivers	Wailua and Waimea rivers on Kaua'i; Wailuku River on Hawai'i; and Kaukonahua Stream on O'ahu, none of them longer than 50 miles (80 km)

Population

Population; rank (2006 estimate):	1,285,498; 42nd
Density (2006 estimate):	200 persons per square mile (77 per sq km)
Population distribution (2000 census):	91% urban, 9% rural
Race (2005 estimate):	Asian persons: 41.5%*
	White persons: 26.8%*
	Native Hawaiian and Other Pacific Islander: 9.0%*
	Black persons: 2.3%*
	American Indian and Alaska Native persons: 0.3%*
	Persons reporting two or more races: 20.1%
	Persons of Hispanic or Latino origin: 8.0%[†]
	White persons not Hispanic: 23.5%

Includes persons reporting only one race.
†*Hispanics may be of any race, so they are also included in applicable race categories.*

Weather

Record high temperature	100°F (38°C) at Pahala on April 27, 1931
Record low temperature	12°F (–11°C) at Mauna Kea on May 17, 1979
Average July temperature	81°F (27°C)
Average January temperature	73°F (22°C)
Average annual precipitation	18 inches (45 cm)

State flag

Hula dancers

STATE SONG

★ ★ ★

"Hawai'i Ponoi" ("Hawai'i's Own People")

The official state song is "Hawai'i Ponoi" ("Hawai'i's Own People"), and it used to be the national anthem of the Kingdom of Hawai'i. It was written in 1874 by King David Kalākaua, with music by Professor Heinrich Berger, the royal bandmaster.

Hawai'i pono'i, Nana i kou moi
Ka lani ali'i, ke Ali'i.
Makua lani e, Kamehameha e,
Na kaua e pale, Me ka ihe.

(translation)
Hawai'i's own true sons, be loyal to your chief
Your country's liege and lord, the Ali'i.
Father above us all, Kamehameha,
Who guarded in the war with his ihe.

Ali'i (ah-lee-ee) means "sovereign."
An ihe (ee-HAY) is a spear.

NATURAL AREAS AND HISTORIC SITES

★ ★ ★

National Parks

Hawai'i has two national parks: the *Haleakalā National Park*, which is home to Haleakalā Crater, endangered species, and scenic pools; and the *Hawai'i Volcanoes National Park*, which stands as the largest national park in Hawai'i, covering 333,000 acres (134,865 ha) and containing the active volcanoes of Mauna Loa and Kīlauea.

National Memorial

Hawai'i's only national memorial is the *USS* Arizona *National Memorial*, which is a floating memorial above the remains of the U.S. battleship sunk during the Japanese raid on Pearl Harbor on December 7, 1941.

National Historic Trail

The Ala Kahakai National Historic Trail, Hawai'i's only national historic trail, offers visitors a beautiful trail marked with significant historical and cultural Hawaiian sites and artifacts.

National Historical Parks

Hawai'i hosts three national historical parks, including the *Kalaupapa National Historical Park*, which is the site of the Moloka'i Island leper colony; the *Kaloko-Honokohau National Historical Park*, which is the site of important settlements from before the arrival of Europeans; and the *Pu'uhonua o Honaunau National Historical Park*, which is the site of sacred grounds from ancient times.

National Historic Site

Hawai'i's sole national historic site, *Pu'ukohola Heiau National Historic Site*, preserves the Pu'ukoholu Heiau, an important religious temple.

State Parks and Forests

Hawai'i has 56 beautiful state parks and recreation areas, including the *Lava Tree State Monument*, *Wailua River State Park*, *Sacred Falls State Park*, and the *Sand Island State Recreation Area*.

SPORTS TEAMS

★ ★ ★

NCAA Team (Division I)

University of Hawai'i at Manoa *Warriors*

The basketball team of the University of Hawai'i at Manoa celebrates a championship

CULTURAL INSTITUTIONS

★ ★ ★

Libraries

Hawaiian Historical Society (Honolulu) houses important state historical documents.

Hawai'i State Library (Honolulu) is the state's largest public library.

University of Hawai'i Library (Honolulu)

Museums

Bernice Pauahi Bishop Museum (Honolulu) concentrates on ethnology and natural history.

Honolulu Academy of Arts (Honolulu) is the state's major art museum, with important collections of Chinese, Japanese, Polynesian, and European art.

Polynesian Cultural Center (Laie on O'ahu) includes seven villages representing the people of Fiji, Hawai'i, Marquesas Islands, New Zealand, the Samoa Islands, Tahiti, and Tonga.

Thomas A. Jaggar Museum (Hawai'i Volcanoes National Park) is a natural history museum.

Performing Arts

Hawai'i has one major opera company.

Universities and Colleges

In 2006, Hawai'i had 10 public and 11 private institutions of higher learning.

ANNUAL EVENTS

January–March

Hula Bowl (college all-star football game) on O'ahu (January)

Hawaiian Open Golf Tournament on O'ahu (January or February)

Narcissus Festival in Honolulu (January or February)

NFL Pro Bowl (February)

Cherry Blossom Festival in Honolulu (February–March)

Kuhio Day (March 26)

April–June

Merrie Monarch Festival in Hilo (March or April)

Lei Day, statewide (May 1)

Kaua'i World Challenge/Annual OC1, OC2, and Surfski Relay Race (May)

50th State Fair on O'ahu (May–June)

Miss Hawai'i Scholarship Pageant in Honolulu (June)

King Kamehameha celebration, statewide (June 11)

July–September

Makawao Rodeo on Maui (July)

Japanese Bon Dances at Buddhist centers (weekends during July and August)

Hawaiian International Billfish Tournament on Hawai'i Island (August)

Keiki Hula Festival in Honolulu (August)

Macadamia Nut Harvest Festival on Hawai'i (August)

Admission Day (August 21)

Hawai'i County Fair in Hilo (September)

October–December

Orchid Plant and Flower Show in Honolulu (October)

Kona Coffee Festival on Hawai'i Island (November)

Hawaiian Pro Surfing on the North Shore of O'ahu (November or December)

Honolulu Marathon in Honolulu (December)

Daniol Kahikina Akaku See page 91.

George R. Ariyoshi (1926–) is the first American of Japanese descent ever elected a state governor. He served as governor of Hawai'i from 1974 to 1986.

Charlotte Fowler Baldwin (1805–1873) reached Hawai'i in 1820 with the fourth group of Protestant missionaries. She helped start schools on the Big Island and kept journals about her experiences.

Helen Kapuailohia Desha Beamer See page 80.

Heinrich Berger (1844–1929) was a bandmaster, arranger, and composer. He wrote the music to Hawai'i's state song, "Hawai'i Ponoi," and helped popularize Hawaiian music.

Hiram Bingham (1789–1869) led the first group of missionaries that went to Hawai'i from New England. He helped to develop a written alphabet for the Hawaiian language.

George R. Ariyoshi

Bernice Pauahi Bishop (1831–1884), a great-granddaughter of Kamehameha I, left money to found the Kamehameha Schools for the education of Native Hawaiians.

Charles Reed Bishop See page 97.

Tia Carrere (born Althea Rae Duhinio Janairo) (1967–) is a singer and film actor born in Honolulu. Her best-known role is that of Sydney Fox in the 1999–2002 television series *Relic Hunter*. She is also the voice of Nani in *Lilo and Stitch*.

Captain James Cook See page 38.

Amos Starr Cooke (1810–1871) was a founder of the company Castle and Cooke Ltd., one of Hawai'i's "Big Five."

Walter F. Dillingham (1875–1963) developed Honolulu's Ala Moana Shopping Center in 1959, the largest in the world at the time of its opening.

Tia Carrere

James Drummond Dole (1877–1958) was the major developer of Hawai'i's pineapple industry. He organized the Hawaiian Pineapple Company, which later became the Dole Pineapple Company.

Sanford Ballard Dole (1844–1926) led the group that seized control of the government from Queen Lili'uokalani in 1893. He headed the Republic of Hawai'i and was appointed to serve as the first governor of the Territory of Hawai'i (1900–1903).

Queen Emma (1836–1885) was the wife of King Kamehameha IV. She led a group of protesters that rioted when David Kalākaua became king.

Hiram Fong (1906–2004) represented Hawai'i in the U.S. Senate from 1959 to 1976. He was the first American of Chinese descent ever elected to the Senate. In Hawai'i, he worked to promote cooperation among the various ethnic groups.

George Freeth See page 81.

Henry Gabriel Ginaca (1876–1918) worked as a mechanical engineer in Honolulu. He invented a machine called a ginaca that peels and cores pineapple.

Sanford Ballard Dole

Jack Wayne Hall (1914–1971) headed the International Longshoremen's and Warehousemen's Union (ILWU). He led a number of successful strikes and helped unionized labor become a powerful force in Hawai'i.

Don Ho (1930–2007) was a singer, storyteller, and comedian whose performances celebrated Hawaiian culture. He was born in Honolulu and grew up in Kaneohe on O'ahu.

Daniel K. Inouye See page 89.

Gerrit P. Judd (1803–1873) went to Hawai'i as a medical missionary and became a major power behind the government of King Kamehameha II.

Laura Fish Judd (1804–1872) was a missionary whose writings are important historical sources about Hawai'i's early missionary years.

Ka'ahumanu See page 45.

Donna Kahakui See page 19.

Don Ho

Duke Paoa Kahanamoku (1889–1968) won gold medals in the 100-yard freestyle competition at the 1912 and 1920 Olympic Games. He held the world record for almost 20 years.

David Kalākaua (1836–1891) was king of Hawai'i from 1874 to 1891. He built 'Iolani Palace, encouraged traditional arts, and was forced to accept the 1887 "Bayonet Constitution" that gave increased power to Hawai'i's sugar planters.

Prince Jonah Kūhiō Kalaniana'ole See page 108.

Kamehameha I See page 41.

Kamehameha II (1797–1824), with the encouragement of his prime minister, Ka'ahumanu, broke the kapu system and allowed Christian missionaries to preach in Hawai'i.

Kamehameha III (1813–1854) was king of Hawai'i from 1825 to 1854. During his reign, he established a legislature and a court system and made possible the private ownership of land.

Kamehameha IV (1834–1863) ruled Hawai'i between 1854 and 1863. He established social and medical programs and tried to limit the power of the American missionaries.

Duke Paoa Kahanamoku

Kamehameha V (1830–1872) ruled Hawai'i from 1863 to 1872. He was the last direct descendant of Kamehameha I to sit on the Hawaiian throne.

Herb Kawainui Kane (1928–) is a painter who spent part of his childhood in Hawai'i, and after studying art at the Art Institute of Chicago, he returned to Hawai'i. Among his books are *Pele: Goddess of Hawai'i's Volcanoes* (1987) and *Ancient Hawai'i* (1998).

John Kidwell (1849?–1922) was a British horticulturist who brought the first pineapple plants to Hawai'i in the 1880s.

Fred Kinzaburo Makino See page 58.

Spark Masayuki Matsunaga (1916–1990) was a veteran of the 100th-442nd Regiment and was elected to the U.S. Senate in 1976.

James A. Michener (1907–1997) was a writer whose novels trace the history of a place through the stories of imaginary people who might have lived there. He moved to Honolulu in 1949, and he completed his novel *Hawai'i* on August 21, 1959—the very day Hawai'i became a state!

Bette Midler (1945–) is a world-famous actress and singer who was born in Honolulu.

Bette Midler

Doris "Dorie" Miller See page 61.

Patsy Takemoto Mink (1927–2002) served as U.S. representative from Hawai'i between 1965 and 1977. She was reelected to the House in 1990 and served there until her death in 2002.

Emma Aima Nawahi See page 52.

Barack Obama (1961–) is a U.S. senator from Illinois. He was born in Honolulu.

Ellison Onizuka (1946–1986) was an astronaut who was a member of the crew of the space shuttle *Challenger* on its tragic final flight.

Kelly Preston (1962–) is a film actor and model who was born and raised in Honolulu.

Graham Salisbury See page 79.

Robert Louis Stevenson (1850–1894) was a famous writer of such novels as *Treasure Island*. He paid two long visits to Hawai'i and publicized Father Damien's work with Hansen's disease patients on Moloka'i.

Barack Obama

Robert R. Taira (1929–2003) was the son of Hawaiian immigrant parents from Japan. He founded the King's Hawaiian Bread Co. in the 1950s.

Lee Tonouchi (1972–) is a writer who promotes the Pidgin language.

Father Damien, Joseph de Veuster See page 111.

Michelle Wie See page 82.

Alan Wong (?–) is a world-famous chef whose dishes combine the flavors of Hawai'i's many cultures.

Robert Wyland (1956–) is a Hawaiian painter noted for his murals of whales and other marine mammals.

Tammy Yee (1946–) is the author and illustrator of many children's books about Hawai'i. Her drawings appear in works such as *A Is for Aloha* and *The Tsunami Quilt*.

Tammy Yee

RESOURCES

BOOKS

Nonfiction

Doak, Robin. *Hawaii: The Aloha State*. Milwaukee: World Almanac Library, 2003.

Kent, Deborah. *Hawai'i's Road to Statehood*. Danbury, Conn.: Children's Press, 2004.

McGowen, Tom. *The Attack on Pearl Harbor*. Danbury, Conn.: Children's Press, 2002.

Obregon, Jose Maria. *Hawai'i*. New York: Power Kids/Buenas Letras, 2005.

Stanley, Fay. *The Last Princess: The Story of Princess Ka'iulani of Hawai'i*. New York: HarperCollins, 2001.

Wade, Mary Dodson. *Tsunami: Monster Waves*. Berkeley Heights, N.J.: Enslow, 2002.

Fiction

McLaren, Clemence. *Dance for the Land*. New York: Atheneum, 1999.

Rumford, James. *Dog-of-the-Sea-Waves: Illustration and Story in English and Hawaiian*. Boston: Houghton Mifflin, 2004.

Salisbury, Graham. *House of the Red Fish*. New York: Wendy Lamb Books, 2006.

Salisbury, Graham. *Under the Blood-Red Sun*. New York: Delacorte Books for Young Readers, 1994.

DVDs

American Experience: Hawaii's Last Queen. PBS/WGBH, 2006.

The Father Damien Story: An Uncommon Kindness. Allumination, 2006.

Globe-Trekker: Hawaii. Pilot Productions, 2004.

Hawaii: Oahu, Maui, Kauai, & the Big Island. Analytical Software, 2005.

Hawaii Songs of Aloha. Mountain Apple, 2002.

Pearl Harbor: Legacy of Attack. National Geographic Video, 2001.

Words, Earth & Aloha: The Source of Hawaiian Music. Hawaiian Legacy Foundation, 2005.

WEB SITES AND ORGANIZATIONS

Hawai'i Department of Natural Resources: State Parks

www.hawaiistateparks.org
Find out more about Hawai'i's 55 state parks.

Hawai'i: The Islands of Aloha

www.gohawaii.com
Find out more about Hawai'i at the state's official travel site.

Hawai'i School Reports

www.Hawaiischoolreports.com
You can find fast facts and information about history, language, nature, and more.

Hawai'i State Government

www.ehawaii.gov/dakine/index.html
At this site, you can find lots of information about the state government and how it runs.

Hawaiian Historical Society

www.Hawaiianhistory.org
This site contains articles and photos about the history of Hawai'i.

Hawaiian Music Hall of Fame

www.hawaiimusicmuseum.org
This site features biographies of traditional Hawaiian musicians.

Hawaiian Roots

www.Hawaiian-roots.com
This site has information to help families trace their Native Hawaiian background

LibrarySpot.com

www.libraryspot.com/state/hi.htm
This site includes maps, government documents, and links to other Hawai'i-related Web sites.

INDEX

★　★　★

AUTHOR'S TIPS AND SOURCE NOTES

★   ★   ★

Many excellent books and Web sites were helpful to me. Two fine histories of Hawai'i are *Hawai'i: An Uncommon History*, by Edward Joesting, and Ruth Tabrah's *Hawai'i: A Bicentennial History.* The Web site of The Hawaiian Historical Society (www.Hawaiianhistory.org) provides a wealth of interesting and useful material. Another valuable resource is the World History Archives site (www.hartford-hwp.com/archives/24/index-a.html), which provides many documents related to the Hawaiian Islands. A great discovery was www.alternative-Hawaii.com. This site is a trove of articles about every aspect of life in Hawai'i, past and present.